"What will an assertive company leader do if the task is to convince an animal to follow them that is five times of their own size and is ready for a flight response at any time? They will get very clear feedback whether they have managed to build trust or not. Being a prey animal and a domesticated species, horses are extremely responsive to human body language. This is what horse-assisted coaching builds on. In order to remind leaders of foundational needs, humans share with animals: 'to be seen, understood and connected'—as Dr Damone puts it in his book."

Dr. Zsófia Virányi *(behavioural biologist), Messerli Research Institute*

"A worthwhile, well-written and insightful book with unique and valuable perspectives. I highly recommend it."

Linda Kohanov, *Author of* The Tao of Equus, The Power of the Herd, The Five Roles of a Master Herder, *and other books on the transformational potential of the horse-human bond*

Leadership Coaching with Horses

Leadership Coaching with Horses offers a transformative approach to leadership development, combining the intuitive power of equine-assisted learning with the precision of biometric technology and psychometric profiling.

This book introduces a pioneering method that harnesses the unique sensitivities of horses alongside advanced biofeedback mechanisms like heart rate variability, providing a comprehensive pathway to enhance personal and professional growth. Delving into the synergistic relationship between humans and horses, this guide details how such interactions foster heightened self-awareness and emotional intelligence. It presents a structured framework for leadership sessions that merge feedback from horses with robust data from biometric and psychometric assessments, enabling a detailed exploration of leadership traits and behaviors and offering measurable outcomes for development.

Distinguished by its novel integration of biometrics and psychometrics into leadership coaching with horses, this book is designed to deepen understanding and enable leaders to make real-time, impactful enhancements to their leadership styles. With practical applications, case studies, and a clear articulation of benefits, it is an essential resource for coaches, HR professionals and leaders seeking innovative, evidence-based tools for advancement.

Dr. Michele Damone, founder of Nature Motivation and a member of the Forbes Coaches Council, inspires leaders and organizations to achieve transformative change. Drawing on his background in criminology and behavioral science, he pioneers groundbreaking coaching strategies that blend biometrics and psychometrics profiling with horse-assisted coaching, empowering leaders to reshape cultures and accelerate growth.

Leadership Coaching with Horses

The Power of Psychometrics and Biofeedback

Dr. Michele Damone

Routledge
Taylor & Francis Group

LONDON AND NEW YORK

Designed cover image: ©Getty Images

First published 2025
by Routledge
4 Park Square, Milton Park, Abingdon, Oxon OX14 4RN

and by Routledge
605 Third Avenue, New York, NY 10158

Routledge is an imprint of the Taylor & Francis Group, an informa business

British Library Cataloguing in Publication Data
A catalogue record for this book is available from the British Library

Library of Congress Cataloging-in-Publication Data
A catalog record has been requested for this book

ISBN: 9781032683850 (hbk)
ISBN: 9781032683836 (pbk)
ISBN: 9781032683843 (ebk)

DOI: 10.4324/9781032683843

Typeset in Times New Roman
by Taylor & Francis Books

Contents

Confirm: Leadership as a Way of Being 132
*Envisioning the Future of Equine-Assisted Leadership
Development 133*

Illustrations

Introduction

The intricate history between humans and horses reveals an integral bond of utility, companionship and mutual benefit that has indelibly shaped the trajectory of humankind. From the moment these magnificent creatures were first domesticated, horses became essential partners along the expansive journey of human civilization. The symbiotic relationship connecting humans and horses over millennia has left an enduring imprint across cultures, accelerated global exploration to new frontiers, and even transformed developments in warfare.

One pioneering philosopher and equestrian who recognized the innate bond between humans and horses was Xenophon of Athens, c. 430–355 BCE, an influential military leader, historian and thinker raised during a turbulent period when common horsemanship practices were overwhelmingly harsh and utilitarian. At that time in history, horses were primarily regarded as transactional tools of war and physical labor rather than the intelligent, emotive beings science reveals them to be today. Training methods enforced dominance through fear, punishment and breaking the horse's spirit to demand compliance rather than building an authentic partnership based on trust and mutual understanding between two species. But true collaboration cannot thrive under such adversarial conditions, no matter how tightly a human might control the outer reins. Thus, societies centered on intensely authoritarian equestrian relationships deprived themselves of reaping the most meaningful benefits of working positively alongside these sensitive creatures' exceptional nature and potential.

Xenophon offered a progressive philosophy that contradicted mainstream attitudes and laid the vital groundwork for empathetic horsemanship, which still strongly resonates through modern coaching approaches partnering with horses centuries later. His revolutionary treatise on horsemanship, penned in the 4th century BCE, emphasized establishing mutual respect, cultivating advanced communication techniques and nurturing genuine understanding as integral foundations necessary between horse and rider for optimal interspecies teamwork. Specifically, Xenophon pioneered several integral concepts:

DOI: 10.4324/9781032683843-1

1   Mutual Respect and Understanding: Xenophon strongly believed a horse would demonstrate increased willingness and ability to perform better if it genuinely respected and trusted its human rider as a fair, compassionate leader. His progressive philosophy shaped foundational concepts that positively reinforced interspecies relationships rather than breaking a horse's spirit to demand compliance. The emphasis on cultivating mutual respect and understanding aligns with modern applications of empathy-based reinforcement techniques, which have been proven to be highly effective for education across animals and humans. When equestrian partnerships build upon positive mutual regard, humans can fully benefit from horses' innate talents while allowing these sensitive beings to thrive. Such collaboration is a significant departure from the authoritarian domination norms of Xenophon's era.

2   Humane Treatment: In a turbulent age when horses were viewed as disposable instruments of war and labor, Xenophon stood out as a vocal advocate for their humane treatment. He championed that horses cared for with patience and kindness would become more willing and able partners, performing duties in agriculture, transportation or even military capacities with increased cooperation. Xenophon recommended the empathy-centered handling of horses, a progressive contrast to the prevalent and ruthless treatment of his times.

3   Effective Communication: Xenophon stressed the immense value of clear, consistent and gentle communication techniques between humans and horses, presaging contemporary double reins models, which prioritizes extremely light-handed rider signaling. He understood a deep appreciation of equine behavioral signals and psychology was mandatory to nurture effective interspecies communication pathways. Thoughtful horsemanship emphasizing advanced communication allows humans to comprehend horse cues better while helping horses better understand human leadership intent, optimizing collaborative potential.

4   Training Principles: Within *On Horsemanship*, Xenophon outlined integral frameworks that are still applicable today, including the necessity of calm, stable settings with patience for skill progression; steady, measured advancement while considering individual horse capability to avoid over-facing or intimidating them; and consistency, thus allowing horses to rely on routines while assimilating new lessons. If these wise training principles are reflected upon, clear parallels also emerge for developing human leadership talents. Gradual measured guidance is most productive for leaders growing their influence upon others. Mutual advancement is best fostered through understanding, kindness, clear messaging and reliably calm direction while incrementally upskilling towards greater goals in a supportive environment.

Moreover, intriguing scientific investigations into early horse domestication patterns and relationships with human civilizations reveal horses' undeniably pivotal role in shaping the trajectory of humankind over millennia. Cutting-edge advances in archaeology, genetics and multidisciplinary research have uncovered compelling insights around domestication, deliberate dispersal and the undeniable bond between humans and horses throughout history. Genetic studies tracing ancestral equine lineages also closely align with known historical distributions of human-horse interaction. Ongoing research highlights correlations between the calculated rising influence of equestrian societies and catalytic linguistic innovations in developing complex vocabularies capable of articulating horseback movements and strategies.[1] The more humanity explores this ages-old relationship, the more the histories of humankind and horses prove to be more undeniably linked.

1   Domestication and Dispersal of Horses: Cutting-edge archaeological discoveries have helped pinpoint the pivotal Eurasian steppes region encompassing modern-day Ukraine, southwest Russia, and west Kazakhstan as the ancient locus where horse domestication originated. Advanced genetic studies tracing morphological changes within ancestral equine DNA over successive eras further bolster the domestication timeline while demonstrating how selectively bred horses were later dispersed worldwide. Analysis reveals a substantial genetic bottleneck occurred, indicating a small number of prized stallions were disproportionately bred, heavily influencing the modern gene pool for deliberate human purposes, like breeding for warhorses.

2   Importance of Historical Patterns: Scientific data demonstrates the calculated dispersal of domesticated horses directly aligns with patterns of human migration and expansionist conquests. Transformational equine attributes provided superior logistics in pivotal areas like transport speed, efficient agriculture and military advantages. Thus, the calculated spread of horses intrinsically intertwined with the expansion of new Indo-European languages through history as migratory equestrian nomadic tribes asserted dominance, assimilating many existing cultures in their wake. Non-equestrian societies could not leverage such overwhelming mobility advantages that horses offered, thus radically accelerating the ascension of horse-mounted peoples over indigenous groups vulnerable to conquest.

3   Horses and Language Development: Beyond vital mobility advantages, horses also directly advanced the evolution in human language through new vocabulary pertaining to equine care and breeding, as well as greater intercultural exposure. Anthropological theories speculate that the rich equestrian lexicon, especially around precise riding cues, facilitated nuanced communication abilities, while horseback mobility enabled extensive interactions between previously isolated human groups. Such unprecedented connectivity and vocabulary exchange inevitably enriched developmental linguistics.

4   Communication Networks: Horses provided far-ranging trade and governance, as they were the essential mobility for messaging relay and logistics chains (like the notable Yam network, which provided necessities such as food and spare horses) that structurally unified the colossal Mongol empire. Without advanced horse-based communication frameworks enabling the projection of military power, diplomatic envoys and rapid information transfer over massive distances, it is impossible to envision any human civilization approaching such vast, contiguous territorial control. The very contours of cities and nations trace infrastructure designed for equine movement. Human development has thoroughly interwoven itself with horses through the millennia.

Moreover, true inspiration lies amid the storied historical relationship between humans and horses, best epitomized by the ancient Roman emperor Marcus Aurelius (121–180 CE). This prominent philosopher and skilled rider intertwined his revered work "Meditations" with astute equestrian metaphors and wisdom, seamlessly blending his deeply reflective leadership ethos with a mastery of both riding and self-discipline. Aurelius artfully utilized equine motifs around control, discipline, balance and overcoming fear, which remain essential across horsemanship today. Furthermore, Marcus Aurelius' immersion into ideals of reasoned passion control while avoiding volatile emotional outbursts mirrors the deliberately calm, confident poise and assertive harmony displayed by the best riders and trainers working safely alongside horses. The alignment between his sage advice on maintaining resolute equanimity amidst adversity and a rider's necessary composure when guiding horses illustrates an enduring interrelation between horsemanship mastery and leadership excellence.

Marcus Aurelius understood that riding was more than mere transportation and saw an opportunity to hone awareness, empathy and communication skills that are indispensable among the most sagacious leaders who transform society. His legacy presaged modern leadership coaching practices based on equine partnerships to unlock latent human potential.

In the saddle, Marcus Aurelius found not just transportation, but a crucible to refine his emotional intelligence and leadership mastery through deepening self-awareness. He recognized the uncanny parallels between mastering a horse and mastering oneself. Just as a rider must grow to comprehend their mount, nurture connection through clear communication and steadily earn equal trust, visionary leaders must similarly devote themselves to understanding, uplifting and earning loyalty among their followers. Marcus Aurelius observed how horses demand sincere vulnerability and authenticity from riders, mirroring their deepest truths. Thus, to him, horses became teachers and therapists, enabling self-realization.

The ancient Romans greatly respected the sophisticated interspecies communication guiding equestrian arts and inherent metaphors bridling the human spirit. Their rich cultural appreciation for horsemanship's practical mobility and personal growth facets revealed enduring insights that the horse-human bond went beyond mere utility when nurtured consciously. Horses were recognized not just as beasts of burden but as complex companions and guides, their emotional sensitivity requiring compassionate collaboration with riders seeking to unlock their potential without coercion. When given patience and empathy, horses are co-therapists in their partners' journeys toward truth, communication excellence and self-mastery. The symbolic unity between rider and mount during competitions also embodied timeless ideals of interspecies harmony, trust and the shared pursuit of grace under pressure, a timeless metaphor carrying deep meaning. The legacy of Marcus Aurelius and ancient equestrian wisdom clearly shows an ageless connection between humans and horses lingering far beyond outward appearances.

This influential connection between humans and horses reached incredible significance within expansive ancient societies heavily reliant upon them, like the Mongols. By coordinating expert horsemanship strategies across far-ranging terrain from the Eurasian steppes to the Danube River plains, Genghis Khan and his armies leveraged lightning mobility to conquer the largest contiguous land empire ever recorded in human history during the 1200s. The very fabric tying together such a vast domain centered on innovative communication and supply lines, which were, by necessity, dependent on their horseback riders. This competitive equestrian edge prompted the rise of an unstoppable nomadic way of life for the Mongols, indelibly shifting the Medieval era's economic and societal trajectories. Compelling archaeological evidence continues to underscore horses' central role in these world-altering civilizations in the Bronze and Iron Ages.[2] Without equine power granting remarkable speed and agility, not to mention sheer distance, while traversing steppe grasslands and high mountain passes, the absolutism and connectivity of the Mongol empire could never have materialized. Truly, no other indigenous creature has similarly revolutionized the capacities and sovereignty of human civilization through partnership as thoroughly as horses.

Following the Middle Ages, the Renaissance further explored this connection between humans and horses, recognizing that the power of this bond extended well beyond an effective means of transportation. Federico Grisone, an Italian riding master and author, made significant contributions to the art of horsemanship during this time period. His treaty, "Gli ordini di cavalcare" (The Rules of Riding), published in 1550, guided aspiring equestrians towards a deeper understanding of their equine partners. Grisone's work emphasized the importance of patience, empathy and clear communication in horse training, principles that align with contemporary approaches to leadership coaching with horses.

The horse-human bond reached an apex during the French Revolution through the legendary partnership between Napoleon Bonaparte and his beloved war stallion, Marengo. This charismatic general keenly appreciated equines' role and forged an unbreakable trust with Marengo as a military champion and dear friend. Named for Napoleon's crucial early 1800 victory, this distinctive grey-white Arabian, that Napoleon rode for 15 years, exemplified resilience and fortitude while bearing his partner into battle after battle, securing France's domination through many arduous campaigns against opposing coalitions.

Most remarkably, at Napoleon's greatest triumph in the infamous three-emperor Battle of Austerlitz, Marengo is said to have carried his rider non-stop upwards of 130 kilometers (roughly 80 miles) from the Czech battlefield all night through a frigid winter storm to the Austrian emperor's palace gates in Vienna by dawn. This astonishing feat, gaining quick access to demand surrender terms, exhibits the sheer degree of Marengo's profound stamina, along with the utmost trust and expert communication between this inter-species team whose very names became legendary. Back home, their bond was similarly inseparable, with Marengo accompanying his renowned rider on long, thoughtful retreats through the countryside in their elder years. Clearly, the exhaustive efforts meticulously documenting, then carefully preserving, Marengo's skeleton for ongoing display indicate Napoleon's immense respect for this mighty steed beyond his riding days. Their enduring alliance in life and through history remains among the most outstanding testaments to the remarkable loyalty and understanding possible between humans and horses.

The modern Lipizzaner breed, regarded for its striking beauty and intelligence, also reflects another pinnacle of selective development in the horse-human bond within the esteemed 18th-century Habsburg Empire and Vienna Spanish Riding School. While originating centuries earlier as sturdy cavalry mounts, attentive stewardship by generations of royals slowly sculpted the Lipizzaner into a vision of power and grace. Under the discerning Emperor Franz's passionate commitment to achieving the ultimate living equine masterpiece, meticulous breeding choices, classical training and unwavering investment in the art of Haute Ecole horsemanship, the Lipizzaners gradually transformed into transcendent embodiments of equine potential equally capable of winning wars or wowing nobility via their movements, sheer elegance and athleticism. By fully nurturing the distinctive talents of their cherished horses as partners over centuries rather than as disposable livestock, the Hapsburgs and their successors at the Spanish Riding School unlocked a depth of splendor, intelligence and rapport between horse and rider, culminating in an equine bloodline that continues inspiring reverence today. This enduring dynasty remains a shining model of understanding horses' hidden talents and selflessly cultivating reciprocal growth.

The legacy of Xenophon, Marco Aurelio, Napoleon, Grisone and the Lipizzaner proves the enduring bond between humans and horses. It's a bond that has evolved over millennia, from the ancient wisdom of Greek philosophers to the refined horsemanship of Renaissance Italy and the regal grace of the Lipizzaner breed. Today, this bond finds new expression in leadership coaching with horses, where the wisdom of the ages meets modern insights into human behavior and personal development.

Benefits of Coaching with Horses in Leadership Development

Horses as Mirrors: A Path to Self-Discovery

One of the foundational advantages of leadership coaching with horses lies in the unique ability of these majestic creatures to act as mirrors, reflecting our inner selves. Horses' role as mirrors is not merely anecdotal—it has a significant basis in neuroscience, mainly through the lens of mirror neurons. Mirror neurons are specialized brain cells that fire when an individual acts, similar to when an individual observes someone else performing that same action. This mirroring effect helps humans learn by imitation, which is fundamental for acquiring new skills and behaviors. Mirror neurons also help us infer the intentions behind others' actions and gain insight into what others are feeling. This is because when we observe someone expressing an emotion, our mirror neurons sometimes lead us to experience a similar feeling. These neurons play a pivotal role in empathy, imitation and understanding the intentions and emotions of others. Remarkably, humans and horses share this neural mechanism.[3]

In leadership coaching with horses, this neural commonality takes on profound significance. Words or façades do not sway horses—they operate authentically based on non-verbal communication. Horses possess finely tuned senses and an uncanny knack for interpreting non-verbal cues. Their ability to discern emotional states and intentions makes them perceptive assessors of human behavior and emotional landscapes[4] with remarkable accuracy, revealing unspoken emotions and intentions.[5] When working with horses, individuals are offered a profound opportunity for self-discovery through mirror neurons. With these inherent abilities, horses can "read" human emotions and intentions, unveiling unspoken thoughts and feelings. The horses respond to this information by reflecting the emotions and intentions they're sensing in their human companions. By noticing and understanding horses' responses, we can gather deeper insight into our subconscious thoughts and feelings, along with the sometimes-obscured reactions of people around us. This mirror-like feedback provides an unfiltered perspective, allowing individuals to witness how their non-verbal signals impact others, echoing the activity of mirror neurons in their brains.[6]

This keen self-awareness becomes a powerful tool in leadership development. It fosters a deeper understanding of interactions with colleagues, team members and friends. As individuals become attuned to their emotional landscapes, they gain insights into their strengths and growth areas. This introspective journey is instrumental in enhancing emotional intelligence, a critical leadership skill. Emotional intelligence enables leaders to navigate complex interpersonal dynamics by using their abilities to recognize, understand and manage their own emotions to perceive and influence the emotions of others. Leaders with high emotional intelligence are better equipped to handle conflict, lead through change and inspire loyalty and engagement from their team members.

The Transformative Journey of Leadership Coaching with Horses

In the evolving leadership coaching landscape, horses have transcended their traditional roles to become powerful partners in transformative coaching journeys. Anchored in the Equine Assisted Growth & Learning Association (EAGALA) Model of Equine-Assisted Psychotherapy, this approach fosters profound personal and leadership growth through activities with horses that facilitate learning via metaphors.[7] Metaphors connect the known with the unknown, enhancing understanding and communication within the therapeutic relationship. They play a pivotal role in creating shared understanding, positively influencing clients' experiences, and fostering adaptability and self-esteem. This process enables clients to explore and reflect upon their thoughts, emotions, behaviors and consequences, empowering them to reframe their perceptions of problems or situations, often leading to innovative solutions and positive therapeutic change.[8]

For example, John experienced a dilemma that's all too common in our modern world. He worked diligently for a company for over a decade, but despite his hard work, he felt unrecognized. His aspirations for leadership seemed increasingly unreachable. He shared his frustration with his coach, who introduced him to the metaphor of the "ladder of success." The coach guided John to envision his career not as a vertical, unscalable wall but as a ladder where each rung represented a skill or relationship to develop.

Through this metaphorical approach, John recognized that he had been waiting passively for someone to notice his value rather than actively climbing the ladder. He began identifying specific "rungs" he had neglected: networking, speaking up about his achievements and seeking mentors. The metaphor transformed John's outlook, allowing him to take control of his progress and create the changes he sought.

Sarah, a leader who struggles with delegation and trust, is another great example. By using leadership coaching with horses to work through these challenges, Sarah could benefit from being blindfolded and asked to lead a horse around an arena, directly experiencing the metaphor of "leading with blind trust." The tactile and immediate feedback from the horse, combined with Sarah's heightened other senses due her inability to see, makes the learning visceral and memorable. She can directly feel the consequences of her actions and the horse's responses, which serves as a powerful metaphor for leadership and trust.

In contrast, traditional executive coaching often applies purely verbal or written metaphor analysis exercises for clients like Sarah, who struggle to delegate control due to underlying trust issues. Coaches may probe her past experiences of feeling out of control while encouraging self-reflection on how those memories influence her current decision paralysis and micro-management tendencies. They could role-play scenarios for practicing delegating tasks without guaranteed outcomes or discuss strategies to consciously build more vulnerability and interdependency within their team. These classic techniques do often provide initial progress through cognitive and emotional levels.

However, leadership development with horses as co-facilitators offers a uniquely immersive learning opportunity to essentially step into the metaphor and feel its intense physical, emotional and social consequences playing out in real-time with a 1000-pound animal ultra-attuned to her every cue. By blindfolding Sarah and guiding unfamiliar horses through intricate courses, this visceral hyperawareness of her body language's impact and the vulnerability of relinquishing control gets etched deeply into memory by activating far more neural networks. The potent combination of adrenaline, earned trust, physical partnership and constant feedback from a horse creates a profoundly personal experience, forging new neural pathways much faster than intellectual discussion alone.

The sheer emotional and physical intensity of collaborating with an alert, high-stakes equine partner while visually impaired leaves an indelible imprint and lifelong reference point for understanding the criticality of clear, confident communication alongside authentic vulnerability. By learning to regulate her emotional state before safely directing these ultra-sensitive horses to mirror her composure, Sarah gains tangible skills for remaining calm under pressure with living beings dependent on her mindfulness. This accelerates transferring insights into daily leadership far more rapidly and comprehensively than cognition allows. The embodied empathy, trust building and follower support skills gained through horse-facilitated learning are unmatched by traditional executive coaching, coaching that simply cannot replicate this level of vulnerability and sincerity. Leadership coaching with horses provides an exponential training multiplier.

Research across broader fields like experiential therapy and psychotherapy underscores the importance of exploring clients' metaphors to comprehend the underlying mindsets behind their actions. In *Leadership Coaching with Horses*, coaches actively listen, craft and evoke metaphors, shedding light on the cognitive, emotional and behavioral aspects of clients' life experiences. To leverage the power of metaphor for insight and change, coaches create a context where participants confront challenges, reflect on difficulties and take responsibility for overcoming obstacles. Clients often engage in role-playing scenarios with horses, practicing skills relevant to real-life issues. Over time, these interactions cultivate mutual trust and respect with the horses, fostering a safe environment conducive to personal growth. Clients are presented with numerous opportunities to acquire and apply new skills, promoting emotional awareness, emotion regulation, self-control and impulse modulation.

Leadership coaching with horses is a dynamic and innovative approach, capitalizing on horses' innate ability to establish profound connections driven by natural curiosity. Celebrated for their non-judgmental and intuitive nature, horses offer individuals authentic interactions that transcend verbal limitations. The horse-human bond is a conduit for fostering emotional intelligence, authentic communication and leadership presence.[9] At the heart of this transformative journey lies the cultivation of emotional intelligence, a cornerstone of effective leadership. This heightened emotional intelligence equips leaders with the empathy and authenticity to navigate complex inter-personal dynamics effectively.[10] An example of how this might play out in a real-world setting is as follows:

Michael, a senior executive at a tech firm, struggled with high turnover in his team. Known for his results-driven approach, Michael often overlooked the impact of his demands on his team's morale. Michael attended a leader-ship development program with horses to improve his leadership skills. Michael was tasked with leading a horse through several obstacles during the program. Initially, he began by trying to direct the horse with the same assertiveness he used at work, including pushing and using power. The horse resisted, unwilling to move forward. The facilitator explained to Michael that horses are sensitive to emotions and respond to genuine connection rather than force. Over time and encouraged to reflect on his behavior, Michael softened his approach, connecting with the horse, stroking its mane and speaking gently. To his surprise, the horse responded positively and coop-erated. Through this interaction, Michael experienced a profound empathy; he recognized that his team needed to feel understood and valued, just like the horse.

Michael returned to work with a renewed focus on understanding his team's perspectives. He began to listen more attentively, acknowledging their stress and challenges. He shared his equine learning experience, expressing his commitment to change. Over time, Michael's increased empathy trans-formed the team dynamic. The team members felt more appreciated and became more engaged, knowing their leader genuinely cared about their well-being. The turnover rate decreased, and the team's productivity and innova-tion soared. Michael's journey became a testament to how emotional intelli-gence, especially empathy and authenticity, can lead to more effective and harmonious interpersonal relationships in the workplace.

The horse-human bond serves as a conduit for authentic communication and developing a powerful leadership presence. Non-verbal communication, a central component of horse interactions, encourages individuals to hone their ability to read and interpret subtle cues. This heightened sensitivity nurtures emotional alignment and the development of empathy, skills that are vital for effective leadership. Moreover, the experiential nature of leadership coaching with horses allows individuals to apply these newfound skills in real-time. Activities that require cooperation and mutual understanding with horses naturally translate into enhanced leadership capabilities. Participants learn to adapt their communication styles, make decisions collaboratively and build strong, cohesive teams, all within the context of their interactions with these perceptive equine partners.

Introduction to Biofeedback Technology and Psychometric Profiling

Integrating biofeedback technology and psychometric profiling into leadership coaching with horses represents a groundbreaking advancement in personal development and emotional intelligence. This innovative approach combines the intuitive insights of equine interactions with the precision and objectivity of biofeedback data and the deep understanding provided by psychometric profiling, creating a powerful synergy that enhances the coaching process.

Biofeedback Technology

Biofeedback technology has significantly advanced our comprehension of the complex interplay between human physiology and emotional states. This innovative technology utilizes physiological data to provide a more in-depth understanding of an individual's emotional and cognitive conditions. Central to this field is the measurement of heart rate variability (HRV), a vital indicator of the autonomic nervous system's functionality.

HRV specifically measures the variation in time intervals between consecutive heartbeats, offering insights that go beyond simple heart rate measurements (beats per minute) to reveal how heart rate fluctuates in response to various stimuli. This variation is crucial as it reflects the dynamic interplay between the sympathetic nervous system, which triggers the body's "fight or flight" response during stress or danger, and the parasympathetic nervous system, which promotes the "rest and digest" state aiding in relaxation and recovery.

The significance of HRV lies in its ability to act as a mirror reflecting an individual's overall autonomic nervous system health and balance. It is sensitive to a range of factors, including emotional stress, physical fitness levels, breathing patterns, sleep quality, general health conditions and even the impact of age. For instance, regular physical activity and a balanced lifestyle enhance HRV by promoting cardiovascular fitness and stress resilience. Conversely, poor sleep quality, unhealthy eating habits, chronic stress and substance use such as alcohol and stimulants can detrimentally affect HRV, indicating an overwhelmed or fatigued autonomic nervous system.

In practical applications, biofeedback through HRV provides a valuable tool for monitoring and improving an individual's emotional regulation and stress management capabilities. By visualizing their physiological responses in real-time, individuals can learn to influence their autonomic functions through controlled breathing, meditation and other mindfulness practices. This form of self-regulation is particularly beneficial in therapeutic settings, helping individuals to manage anxiety, depression and stress-related disorders more effectively.

Moreover, HRV biofeedback is increasingly used in various professional fields, including sports science, where athletes leverage this data to optimize their training and recovery processes. It helps in identifying the optimal balance between training intensity and rest, ensuring that athletes do not over-train and have adequate recovery to perform at their best.

The broader implications of biofeedback extend to everyday life and workplace settings, where HRV monitoring can guide individuals in managing their day-to-day stress and promoting a healthier, more balanced lifestyle. Organizations are beginning to adopt biofeedback tools as part of wellness programs to help employees manage stress and enhance overall productivity and well-being.

HRV has garnered significant attention in research due to its close association with emotional regulation and stress management.[11] Scientific studies have consistently demonstrated that HRV is a reliable indicator of an individual's ability to adapt to stress, with higher HRV values being associated with better emotional regulation and resilience.[12]

Psychometric Profiling

Psychometric profiling is a sophisticated method that employs a variety of assessments designed to measure and analyze an individual's psychological attributes. These attributes encompass personality traits, cognitive abilities and behavioral tendencies, offering a comprehensive view of a person's psychological landscape. The use of these assessments provides valuable insights into an individual's characteristic ways of thinking, feeling and behaving, which are essential in understanding oneself and in facilitating personal and professional growth.

These tools are particularly useful in settings where understanding individual differences is key to optimizing group dynamics, such as in workplaces, educational environments and therapeutic settings. By providing a detailed profile of an individual's personality traits, cognitive strengths, potential areas for development and overall leadership capabilities, psychometric assessments can guide coaches, educators and therapists in tailoring their interventions more effectively.

For coaches and mentors, psychometric profiling is an indispensable tool. It helps in identifying the inherent strengths and potential blind spots of their clients. Coaches can use this information to better structure their coaching sessions, focusing on leveraging the client's strengths while also addressing and improving areas that require development. This targeted approach not only accelerates personal development but also enhances the effectiveness of coaching in achieving desired outcomes.

Furthermore, psychometric assessments can provide leaders with insights into their own leadership styles, helping them understand how they are likely to react under stress, how they make decisions, and how they interact with others in a leadership capacity. This self-awareness is critical in helping leaders refine their approach to managing teams, resolving conflicts and leading effectively.

For example, an assessment reveals that Jordan, a team leader, has high analytical abilities and is detail-oriented, but tends to be risk-averse and has difficulty adapting. These traits suggest that while Jordan is excellent at strategic planning and critical analysis, he might struggle in fast-paced or unpredictable situations where quick decision-making is crucial. With this understanding, a coach might work with Jordan to leverage his strengths in planning to create more flexible strategies that account for potential changes. The coach could introduce exercises that simulate unexpected scenarios, encouraging Jordan to use his analytical skills to evaluate the situation and make quick decisions. The coach might also encourage Jordan to practice delegation, trusting others to handle some details. This would help Jordan develop more adaptability and build a more empowered and dynamic team. By using his inherent strength in analysis, Jordan can create a framework that allows for flexibility and helps overcome his aversion to risk.

Integration of Biofeedback and Psychometric Profiling

The innate sensitivity of horses to non-verbal emotional cues during experiential activities offers leadership coaching participants an invaluable mirror into their internal landscapes. By subtly reflecting the true feelings and stress levels they sense from humans through slight behavioral reactions, horses provide immediate, honest biofeedback into how one's underlying emotional states impact others—a foundational pillar of self-awareness essential for leadership roles.

This equine sensitivity is seamlessly integrated with technological and psychological assessments to create a uniquely comprehensive evaluation of a leader's emotional and cognitive functions. For instance, biofeedback sensors can objectively track physiological stress reactions, such as an elevated heart rate, as a participant approaches an unfamiliar horse. At the same time, psychometric tools measure inherent psychological attributes like risk tolerance. These quantitative insights, when combined with the qualitative feedback from the horse—such as behavioral signals like a tucked tail or neck tension—paint a vivid picture of the anxiety induced by the leader's presence.

By merging the intuitive feedback from equine interactions with the quantifiable data provided by biosensors and personality assessments, participants are afforded a holistic view of their emotional regulation capacities and psychological traits. This integration allows for a multidimensional exploration of how emotional, physical, and personality factors intertwine and influence leadership behaviors. Participants gain deep self-insight about their intrinsic habits and triggers, while coaches receive a rich amalgam of visible data points, enabling them to provide personalized and precise guidance.

Furthermore, this approach enhances the overall effectiveness of leadership development programs by offering a dual perspective: the internal, reflective insights provided by psychometric assessments, and the external, reactive observations made possible through biofeedback and equine feedback. Such a dynamic and interactive method fosters a deeper understanding of self that is crucial for effective leadership, helping individuals not only recognize but also learn to manage their emotional responses in real-time.

This integrated methodology essentially bridges the gap between personal development's emotional, physiological and psychological facets to promote significantly accelerated transformation within the leadership coaching with horses context. With deepened self-understanding, clients gain practical biofeedback skills for recognizing turbulent stress responses earlier and modulating unhelpful reactions in real-time before negative habits manifest— creating composed, agile leaders. Horses even model self-regulation by moving in sync with their human partner's state through attunement exercises. Overall, this groundbreaking approach leverages multidimensional data tracking alongside horses' natural emotional mirroring capacity to equip leaders with unprecedented self-mastery during uncertainty.

Embracing the Future: Exploring New Frontiers

As the epic journey of leadership coaching alongside horses continues to evolve, our collective horizon expands to encompass thrilling new possibilities grounded in ancient wisdom, but guided by visionary scientific advancements. The initial integration of real-time biofeedback and personality assessments represents the first step on a truly revolutionary path toward unlocking the full transformation potential hidden within the remarkable horse-human connection. This book sets the stage for a new era of holistic personal growth, embracing the intuitive magic and measurable science behind this interspecies partnership. By blending data-driven technologies measuring stress responses, personality traits and more alongside thoughtful customization of metaphorical horse interactions, a powerful synergy emerges that unlocks far deeper personal insights than either realm could unveil independently. As this personalized approach leveraging precise bio-tracking and meaningful equine engagement advances further, vast new frontiers open for humanity to strengthen emotional intelligence, resilience, empathy and communication skills unlike any other methodology conceived.

This book comprises five chapters, each addressing what the author identifies as the most critical and occasionally counterintuitive aspects of coaching with horses, alongside biometrics and psychometrics profiling. While these chapters are interrelated, they are designed to function independently, allowing readers to engage thoroughly with each distinct element of this innovative methodology.

The time has arrived to collectively expand our notion of what is possible, innovatively building upon the ancient roots of horse-human understanding while courageously integrating ever-improving technologies and new, forward-thinking paradigms. As visionary leadership coaches increasingly integrate these comprehensive skillsets, their clients gain access to unprecedented self-actualization breakthroughs surpassing traditional limitations. Ultimately, by embracing the future of this work as the growth frontier it represents, the field of equine-assisted development unquestionably takes decisive steps toward unlocking the revolutionary, transformative potential within leaders, teams and organizations worldwide for generations to come. Our shared journey of insightful possibility in symbiotic partnership with these extraordinarily sentient teachers has just begun.

Notes

1 Bennett, D. (1998). *Conquerors: The roots of new world horsemanship.* Amigo Publications.
2 Anthony, D. W. (2007). *The horse, the wheel, and language: How Bronze-Age riders from the Eurasian steppes shaped the modern world.* Princeton University Press.
3 Rizzolatti, G., Fogassi, L., & Gallese, V. (1996). Functional MRI evidence for mirror neuron activity in the human brain. *Neuron,* 13(2), 375–382.
4 Kohanov, L. (2003). *The Tao of Equus: A woman's journey of healing and transformation through the way of the horse.* New World Library.
5 De Benedittis, A., Marazziti, D., Mandarelli, G., & Lac, V. (2021). Exploring the effects of equine-assisted psychotherapy: A systematic review. *Animals,* 11(2), 487.
6 Jones, J. L. (2008). *Horse brain, human brain: The neuroscience of horsemanship.* Trafalgar Square Books.
7 EAGALA. (2012). *Fundamentals of EAGALA model practice untraining manual* (7th ed.). Equine Assisted Growth and Learning Association.
8 Reisfield, G. M., Wilson, G. R. (2004). Use of metaphor in the discourse on cancer. *Journal of Clinical Oncology,* 22(19). https://doi.org/10.1200/JCO.2004.03.136.
9 Bachi, K. (2016). *Horse sense for leaders: Building trust-based relationships.* Triarchy Press.
10 Slayton, S. C., Bozentka, A. B., & Petersen, N. S. (2016). Equine-assisted psychotherapy: A descriptive study. *Journal of Creativity in Mental Health,* 11(1), 104–116.

11 Laborde, S., Mosley, E., & Thayer, J. F. (2017). Heart rate variability and cardiac vagal tone in psychophysiological research: Recommendations for experiment planning, data analysis, and data reporting. *Frontiers in Psychology,* 8, 213.

12 Thayer, J. F., & Lane, R. D. (2000). A model of neurovisceral integration in emotion regulation and dysregulation. *Journal of Affective Disorders,* 61(3), 201–216.

Chapter 1

Foundations of Leadership Coaching with Horses

Humans are social creatures with a deep-seated need to connect, belong and gain the approval of their peers, which are critical for our survival. Much like humans, horses communicate through their internal feelings and intuitive senses. The safety of the herd depends on each member's ability to sense danger from predatory animals. Predatory animals, including humans, hold stress in their bodies. This stress not only creates a different physical posture but also a particular chemistry and smell. Horses are tuned into these levels of information and can quickly identify another animal with predatory intentions. They sense when they need to move away from danger and when it is safe to graze. Horses communicate with each other through their feelings and reactions. When one horse becomes nervous and instinctively moves to safety, the whole herd moves together as if they share the same knowledge of consciousness.

Because of this instinct to avoid being prey to other animals, including humans, horses are finely attuned to incongruences in human states of being that we often overlook. For example, a leader may approach a horse feeling anxious but attempting to appear confident and self-assured. Though they adopt a strong posture, the horse detects subtle physical tension cues—a quickened heartbeat, taut muscles, shallow breathing—that reveal the leader's hidden unease. Despite the veneer of confidence, the horse mirrors the leader's true tentative emotional state, hesitating to engage, while keeping a wary distance. Additionally, if a leader's body language conveys uncertainty or distraction that contradicts the certainty of their verbal commands, the horse may not respond as expected, detecting the misalignment between intentions and actions. By reflecting our unconscious tension and mismatched intentions through their reactions, horses hold up a mirror that makes visible what we fail to see in ourselves. Leadership coaching with horses provides a wake-up call, balancing our tendency to over-rely on thinking by tuning into the wisdom of our sensing energy and emotions. Working with these highly sensitive animals catalyzes greater self-awareness, authenticity and wholeness—foundational to truly transformational leadership. By learning to read horses, we learn to read ourselves better.

DOI: 10.4324/9781032683843-2

Horses can sense emotions and intentions that humans often overlook or fail to detect within themselves. Horses have evolved to be highly attuned to their environment and aware of potential threats. This instantaneous responsiveness aligns with the principles in Daniel Kahneman's *Thinking, Fast and Slow* (2011),[1] where a horse's thinking is described as a duality between fast, intuitive thinking and slow, deliberate reasoning. Their survival depends on an innate capacity to read subtle cues signaling danger or deceit. As a result, horses offer invaluable insights for leadership development, acting as catalysts for greater self-awareness and emotional intelligence. When working with horses, leaders quickly discover that hiding or suppressing emotions is futile. Horses immediately react to these inconsistencies between a person's outer presentation and their inner state. If a leader projects confidence but secretly feels insecure or pretends to be happy when frustrated, horses become unsettled and resist engagement. *Like predator and prey in the wild, a misalignment in energy triggers distrust.* For horses to feel safe and connected, leaders must be authentically aligned in mind and body.

Horses provide pure, unfiltered feedback devoid of the complexities of human psychology. They do not consciously judge or interpret. Rather, horses rely on their intuitive *"body-brain,"* reacting viscerally to a leader's energy and intentions. This makes horses exceptionally adept at mirroring leadership behaviors, reflecting tendencies that may limit effectiveness. With horses, the false veneer of leadership gives way to its truer essence. The dynamic insights gleaned from equine interactions transfer directly to leadership growth. Just as horses demand consistency, human teams perform best when a leader's words align with their disposition. *No amount of charisma can mask unresolved fear, anxiety, frustration or anger.* Horses detect and reflect these states immediately. Being aware of a horse's reactions teaches leaders to recognize their impact on others. It is a profound lesson in self-awareness.

Beyond emotional awareness, horses also highlight leadership through non-verbal communication. Herd dynamics offer meaningful metaphors for team leadership. How a leader enters the horses' space, establishes presence and engages the group provides powerful lessons about authority, influence, trust-building and motivation that apply directly to leading people. Subtleties in movement, positioning and energy convey as much as the words spoken from human to horse. For authentic development, time with horses alternates between periods of action and periods of reflection. In-the-moment experiences create visceral impressions, which are processed consciously through coaching conversations. As perspectives shift, new approaches can be tested. With repetition, a leader's consciousness expands, embodiment deepens and new habits crystallize. *It is an iterative process of experimentation, feedback, reflection and integration.*

Leadership coaching with horses is about uncovering wholeness within the leader and between the leader and the team. Horses only respond favorably to human partners who can access a mindset of security and benevolence. This requires leaders to examine and resolve inner fears, insecurities or control tendencies that block trust-based relationships. Horses quickly bring unresolved emotional baggage to the surface, insisting on inner work as a prerequisite for outer influence. The horse-human dynamic also illuminates the sacred responsibility of leadership itself. Evaluating oneself honestly, regulating emotions skillfully, establishing trust and motivating others positively – these capabilities nurture growth within the team. Horses will only partner with compassionate leaders seeking to uplift the collective. Anything less leads to resistance and dissent. In this, horses provide the model for inspired leadership that unlocks potential and honors dignity. Their wisdom helps leaders understand power as service, not domination.

Through developing body-brain awareness and heart-centered relationships, leaders gain access to the innate attributes that build resonant teams: authenticity, emotional intelligence, empathy and care. These capacities transcend technique or credentials. They arise from within, are cultivated through self-mastery and are nourished in the community. Horses guide leaders on this journey with sensitivity, providing a safe space to rediscover core humanity and to lead from there. Leadership coaching with horses in practice unfolds as a graceful dance between humans, horses and nature. Sessions occur on the horses' turf, often on a ranch or farm setting. This immersive experience invites leaders into a new sensory awareness beyond traditional coaching rooms. Leaders are briefed on safety procedures and basic horse psychology to ensure smooth interactions. Reputable programs partner leaders with horses who enjoy human contact and learning together.

Prior to meeting the horses, the coach will help the leader set intentions for the session. They will discuss what skills or emotional capacities they want the horses to illuminate and how ready the leader is to receive candid feedback. These reflections focus on the process for maximum impact. The initial encounter emphasizes relationship building through mutual trust and respect. Approaching calmly, reading horse body language, allowing them choice and agency in interactions—these actions form the foundation of secure attachment. Wonderful lessons about adjusting power dynamics, earning consent and truly "meeting another" apply directly to leadership.

Once rapport is established, the coach guides the leader through experiential activities to reveal particular capabilities. For example, having the leader guide their horse over obstacles teaches influence through caring direction, not force. If the horse refuses, the leader adapts their approach based on feedback. Direct parallels exist between motivating people and "*managing*" a 1000-pound animal. The horse responds to the leader's presence and actions throughout each activity through their behavior and body language. The coach helps the leader interpret these signals as valuable insights for development. If the horse seems anxious, the coach will determine what the leader is transmitting unconsciously. If the horse ignores certain directions, the leader must determine what this conveys about their authority. The horses' spontaneous reactions reveal dynamics that discussions alone often miss.

There are also powerful lessons in simply sharing space with such large, powerful creatures. Horses invite leaders to manage their emotions skillfully to co-create safety. Their size demands care and compassion in relating. Leaders must regulate their energy to allow the horses to reciprocate. Being fully present with such sensitive beings builds emotional intelligence rapidly.

The coach and leader will pause to integrate insights through reflective discussion at intervals. The coach poses questions to help the leader examine patterns illuminated with the horses and relate them to their leadership. Together, they discuss strategies to align words and actions, lead authentically, earn trust and motivate positively. They explore how working with an intuitive horse reveals blind spots in relating to people. These "aha" moments represent touchstones for development. Turning fresh discoveries into conscious leadership practice allows new behaviors to emerge. The coach's questions prompt consideration of integrating heightened sensitivity, care and emotional mastery into daily leadership beyond the horse setting. In this way, horses hold up a mirror, but humans must internalize what they see and intentionally develop their skills from there.

Shared reflection also replenishes energy and focus, allowing leaders to approach subsequent activities with renewed purpose. There is wisdom in balancing action with reflection, as leadership integrates both being and doing. Coaching conversations around the horse work enable continuous growth through experience, inquiry and integration cycles. In total, sessions with horses strip leadership back to the core human values of integrity, compassion and service. The masks leaders often wear melt away, revealing who they are underneath. It is a journey of self-actualization, accelerated by the clarity and honesty that horses bring. Their ancient wisdom empowers leaders to fulfill their highest purpose—serving the greater collective through actualizing their best selves. Leadership coaching with horses integrates four key developmental elements:

1   Experiential learning in partnership with horses
2   The horses' honest reactions provide real-time feedback and mirroring for self-improvement
3   Guided discussions to interpret experiences and extract leadership lessons
4   Ongoing integration to implement insights into improved emotional, relational and team leadership capabilities

This process unfolds over a series of sessions, enabling incremental growth through layers of progressive mastery. Leaders build emotional intelligence, cultivate presence and resonance, and actualize care-based authority. Horses accelerate development by demanding truth-in-action and responding accordingly. Their feedback cuts through pretense right to the heart of real influence. Fundamentally, horses reveal leadership that fulfills its highest purpose—bringing out the best in others through first grounding personal mastery. They mirror integrity, insist on care and refract ego into service. Leaders unable to demonstrate these qualities will find no cooperation from their equine teachers. Only when humans approach horses with humility, empathy and reverence for their wisdom can connection flourish. This points to the deeper, regenerative impact possible when leading from presence. Horses model gentle strength from inner security, sensitivity and calm. They embody leadership as service, dedication to the well-being and actualization of the herd. When humans embrace this ethos, teams thrive organically through inspiration rather than control. The horses remind leaders that caring deeply for people's growth is the heart of great leadership.

In the rush of daily responsibilities, it is easy for leaders to lose touch with foundational human needs—to be seen, understood and connected. When disconnected from these basics, leadership suffers. Strategies and tactics lose resonance. Teams splinter from misalignment between speech and spirit. Horses call leaders back to emotional integrity as the antidote. Their ancient wisdom restores core human values to leadership in a profound, experiential way. Of course, acting from presence remains an ideal that we asymptotically approach but never fully attain. That is why recurring experiences with horses prove so valuable. Each session reveals more layers to be explored and integrated over a lifetime. Leadership mastery is not a destination but an ongoing journey of growth. Equine teachers walk this path with us, bringing healing and hope when needed.

Even a single coaching session with horses yields powerful insights, planted like seeds in a leader's consciousness. Under conducive conditions, these seeds germinate into new behaviors and elevated leadership. But the deepest transformations occur through sustained engagement with horses over months and years. Each encounter builds upon those before, creating a qualitative shift that compounds gradually like drops filling a well. In this way, horses become guides accompanying leaders on the adventure of actualizing their highest self in service to their organizations.

There is both magic and pragmatism in this. On the surface, people play with horses, laugh together and share space. Yet through relationships with these sensitive creatures, leaders gain access to parts of themselves often obscured by the fog of thought and time's hurried pace. Being with horses, like being with all nature, reconnects humans to timeless sources of meaning within. Leadership grounded in this humility cannot help but uplift others. And so we return full circle to the premise upon which this journey rests— *leadership mastery flowers from inner mastery, achieved through practices that reveal and actualize one's highest self.* Horses accelerate and condense this fact, demanding we shed all pretense and meet them in presence to earn cooperation. They respond to our most authentic core and ignore anything less. This makes horses uncompromisingly effective mirrors for leadership development.

By reflecting our inner terrain through unfiltered, intuitive senses, horses shed light on blind spots and expedite conscious leadership growth. Their ancient wisdom helps modern leaders strip away distracting artifice and reconnect with foundational human values channeled into noble service. Leadership coaching with horses offers an experience of our collective potential, waiting patiently for us to walk in cadence with life's underlying rhythms once again.

The Horse as a Mirror: Reflections of Leadership Behaviors

As mentioned earlier, horses possess an extraordinary aptitude for reading human emotions and intentions through subtle non-verbal cues. This ability offers invaluable opportunities for leadership development, as time spent interacting with horses can rapidly enhance self-awareness, emotional intelligence, communication skills and relationship building. Horses provide pure, unfiltered feedback by reflecting a leader's inner state through spontaneous reactions and body language. If a leader projects confidence but hides self-doubt or anxiety, horses become unsettled and resist direction. Horses cooperate fully when a leader's outer composure aligns with their inner disposition. This candid mirroring teaches leaders the importance of emotional authenticity for earning trust and influence.

A key driver of horses' sensitivity is that, as prey animals, their survival has always depended on detecting predator threats. Horses are conditioned to analyze risks and intentions through subtle cues like scent, body language and tone of voice. They will instinctively flee from humans exhibiting aggression or deceit. This makes horses exceptional judges of character and emotional honesty. Horses also possess highly attuned non-verbal communication skills. They synchronize behaviors and intentions through subtle cues that humans can scarcely detect. This non-verbal fluency is enabled by mirror neurons, specialized brain cells that activate when performing and observing an action. Mirror neurons allow horses to empathize and share collective knowledge of their environment.

For leaders, interacting with horses provides an opportunity to experience leadership stripped of words, titles and other trappings. Horses follow energy, presence and authentic intent. They instantly notice inconsistencies between a leader's outward comportment and underlying emotional state, providing unfiltered feedback about the leader's integrity and impact. This candid mirroring accelerates self-awareness and growth. Beyond emotional intelligence, horses offer teachings around asserting leadership presence and earning consent. Approaching horses calmly, reading their cues, and building trust fosters care-based authority. Herd dynamics also illuminate team leadership, with the horse group responding to how confidently and benevolently the human provides direction. Horses only cooperate with leaders focused on collective well-being. Equine-assisted development unfolds through experiential learning cycles, coached reflection and integration. Hands-on activities with horses create visceral learning moments. Coaching conversations help leaders process insights and relate them to improving human leadership. Over time, emotional mastery and care-based authority become ingrained through this iterative practice. Scientific studies endorse the effectiveness of equine-assisted development:

1   Research finds that mirror neurons enable horses to empathize with human emotions. This allows horses to provide candid feedback by responding to a leader's underlying disposition, not just outward behaviors.
2   Studies show that interacting with horses enhances leaders' emotional intelligence, self-awareness and social skills. Horses demand authenticity and connection, illuminating blind spots.
3   Neuroscience confirms that shared neural circuits for perception and action facilitate the interspecies communication underlying horse-human leadership development.
4   Psychology research reveals that equine therapy improves psychological well-being, confidence and social functioning. Partnership with horses creates a safe space for healing and growth.[2]

Navigating Space, Energy and Timing

Entering the horse's space creates opportunities to learn core lessons around presence, boundaries and consent.

Spatial Dynamics

- Horses have defined flight zones—invasions causing stress. Approach indirectly, allowing choice.
- Their visual fields require slow, wide movements around the horse. Sudden approaches risk triggering flight response.
- Positioning shows leadership—being centered and facing the group exudes confidence and care.

Energy

- Horses read and mirror human emotions like fear, anxiety or anger through shifts in posture, scent and vocal tones.
- Remaining calm with grounded, focused energy provides comfort and earns cooperation.

Timing

- Horses communicate through precise temporal behaviors (e.g., ear twitches, foot stomps). Humans must tune into these rhythms.
- Matching the horse's tempo shows empathy. Rushing overwhelms; patience allows trust.

With care, awareness and understanding, the horse's space becomes a classroom for strengthening emotional intelligence and care-based leadership presence. These lessons translate directly into human teams.

The Mirror Effect: How Horses Accelerate Leadership Growth

Equine therapies leverage the horse's innate sensitivity and non-verbal communication skills to provide a mirror for human development. Horses respond in each moment to a leader's energy and intentions, delivering rapid feedback for improved emotional mastery, presence and relationship building. Leaders gain perspective about their perceptions by working directly with these sensitive creatures. Horses offer unfiltered insights around authenticity, trust-building, motivation and managing distress. Interacting with a 1000-pound animal quickly exposes weak spots, fears or manipulative tendencies undermining leadership.

With guidance, leaders reflect on patterns illuminated in horse engagement and relate those patterns to their human leadership. Coaching conversations help extract lessons about better relating to colleagues through heightened empathy, vulnerability and alignment. This experiential learning cycle, coached reflection and integration imprints new leadership habits over time. The horse's candid feedback provides a fast track for enhancing self-awareness, and relating horse behavior to human dynamics builds emotional and social intelligence rapidly. Some specific areas where horse mirroring accelerates leadership growth include:

1 Authenticity—Horses demand congruency between inner and outer states. This teaches leaders that pretenses undermine trust and morale.
2 Presence—Approaching horses with confident, centered energy earns cooperation. This translates to engaging teams authoritatively.
3 Influence—Horse compliance depends on clear, compassionate direction, not force. Leaders learn positive persuasion.
4 Self-Regulation—Remaining calm and focused when horses become reactive teaches critical emotional control.
5 Empathy—Reading subtle horse cues builds the ability to sense others' unspoken needs and emotions.

Equine-assisted development compresses years of leadership growth into tangible lessons through horse interactions. The horse's immediate, unfiltered feedback cuts through the blindness people often have about themselves. By integrating insights gained working with horses, leaders rapidly amplify their emotional, social and team intelligence.

Leadership Principles Reflected in Horse Herd Dynamics

Observing horses interact provides powerful metaphors for team leadership. Horse herd structures and dynamics also offer lessons around authority, social roles, motivation and collective purpose.

Herd Hierarchy

- Herds have organized hierarchies for safety. More experienced members mentor youngsters.
- Leaders earn authority by proving competence, not domination. Security arises from cooperation.

Social Roles

- Group roles like a lead horse, sentinel and nurturer align abilities for the herd's cohesion and well-being.
- Leadership is situational—roles adapt to changing needs. The position serves the whole.

Motivation

- Horses share collective knowledge and synchronize behaviors to protect the group. Each contributes personal strengths.
- Effective leaders awaken intrinsic team motivation by connecting work to purpose and potential.

By observing herd interactions, leaders gain perspective about structuring cohesive, productive teams through cooperation, not compliance. Horse social dynamics distill empowering leadership principles that transfer directly into human systems.

The Heroic Journey: Leadership as Inner Discovery

At its core, equine-assisted leadership development ignites a heroic inner journey toward self-actualization. Working with horses accelerates this awakening, demanding leaders shed their armor of pretense and approach horses with authentic vulnerability as the path to partnership. By reflecting their rawest, truest selves, horses reveal the work required to unleash their highest potential. Their feedback exposes fears, insecurities and blind spots as grist for the wheel of transformative growth. They celebrate progress while insisting on continual self-examination. This process unfolds through four main stages of increasing wisdom:

1   Unconscious Incompetence: Leaders start this process unaware of how their inner landscape impacts horses and leadership. Blind spots abound.
2   Conscious Incompetence: The horse's responses create "aha" moments, revealing new self-insights. Awareness expansions beg integration.
3   Conscious Competence: Leaders intentionally apply emotional skills gained with the horses to lead human teams more effectively.
4   Unconscious Competence: New leadership practices integrate fully. Wisdom gleaned from horses becomes second nature.

Each stage builds on the last through repeating cycles of experiential learning and inner work. Initial breakthroughs yield deeper transformations over months and years. Like peeling an onion, layers of old patterns get revealed and shed. Negative emotions once suppressed are now embraced for the wisdom within, and reactivity gives way to centered strength. Leadership authority flows authentically from core values like courage, compassion and service as the true self emerges. This heroic journey transforms leadership on a soul level and hardened masks crack open to reveal leaders' fundamental humanity. Connecting to this vulnerable core empowers new leadership built on self-awareness, emotional mastery and care for the collective. Resistance and domination give way to aligned authority. Horses demand this inner work as the price of cooperation. They respond only to human partners who embody their highest selves in service to the herd. Any residual ego or toxicity gets mirrored instantly in the horse's distrust. This, in turn, motivates leaders to keep examining the unconscious and continually renew their wholeness. Engaging in this honest self-reflection is challenging yet essential, and the horse's feedback provides a compass through the inner terrain. Their wisdom separates authentic aspirations from ego desires. Leaders gain strength by listening deeply to horses to walk the heroic path to wholeness.

The Inner Journey's Outward Rewards: Leadership Renewed

The inner discoveries enabled by horse wisdom manifest gradually as positive shifts in a leader's emotional intelligence, presence and relationships. For example:

- Leaders remain composed under stress, regulating emotions for optimal impact.
- They exude a confident presence while inviting participation and co-creation.
- Teams feel genuinely seen, valued and empowered by aligned leadership.
- Conflicts are resolved through empathetic listening and leveraging collective insights.

- Vulnerability and intuition balance analytical decision-making.
- Leaders uplift others through heart-centered relationships.

These ongoing benefits illustrate leadership originating from inner mastery and fulfillment. By reflecting leaders' deepest truths, horses empower this transformation from reactive management to visionary service. Leadership becomes not a title but a way of interacting that activates potential—authority stems from modeling integrity and purpose. Serving people's growth eclipses ego needs and leaders fully embody their empowering essence. The effects of this integrative leadership radiate through teams like water-nourishing thirsty roots. Renewed leaders see gifts in each person and unite diverse talents to achieve shared visions, with people feeling safe to express ideas and passions. As teams blossom, they draw out greatness in their communities.

This systemic influence reminds leaders that inner shifts create outer change. The seminal work is not in grand strategies, but in small moments of being fully present, leading from the heart and offering empathy. Little by little, these human touches compound into vibrant cultures where every voice matters. By walking the inner path with courage and humility, leaders gain the wisdom to lead others with grace. This is the sacred covenant horses help fulfill. Their ancient mastery becomes our secret ally for growth. For those willing to accept the horse's mirror and honor their teachings, a world of possibility awaits. Leadership grounded in wholeness flows from essence to form in ripples without end.

Non-Verbal Communication and Emotional Resonance

Non-verbal communication is the backbone of the interaction between horses and humans. For both species, communication extends far beyond words, with non-verbal cues playing a pivotal role in conveying emotions, intentions and states of being. It's estimated that up to 70% of human communication is non-verbal, highlighting the immense significance of this form of interaction in our daily lives. With their remarkable sensitivity, horses excel in perceiving and interpreting these non-verbal signals. They are finely tuned to human emotions, capable of discerning even the subtlest shifts in energy and emotional states. This heightened perception is not limited to positive emotions; horses are equally adept at detecting signs of stress and discomfort. This acute sensitivity is rooted in their ancient role as prey animals, where the ability to swiftly recognize potential danger from predatory animals was a matter of life and death.

Numerous scientific studies have shed light on the extent of horses' ability to respond to changes in human physiology and body language. These studies have revealed that when a human's emotional state lacks alignment, horses readily detect the incongruences, triggering corresponding shifts in their behavior. They become mirrors of human emotional resonance, unveiling areas of discord within human participants. Studies demonstrate that horses can differentiate between happy and angry human expressions and alter their behavior accordingly, showcasing a clear response to the emotional valence of a human facial expression.

One particularly telling study involved horses being presented with photographs of human faces expressing different emotions. The horses showed increased heart rates and more stress-related behaviors when viewing angry faces compared to happy ones.[3] This physiological response suggests that horses not only perceive human emotions but are also affected by them, a phenomenon likely underpinned by the mirror neuron system, which is thought to be involved in empathy and social understanding in humans.[4] In one instance, a therapy horse named Bella was paired with a young man struggling with anxiety. Initially, the man attempted to mask his anxious feelings, presenting a stoic façade. However, Bella remained distant and agitated, pacing around the arena's edge as she sensed his hidden anxiety. The facilitators encouraged the man to acknowledge his feelings openly, explaining that as he did so, Bella's behavior would reflect this. As he began to express his anxiety, his physiological signals—likely his heart rate and breathing—changed, becoming more congruent with his verbal acknowledgment of fear.

Remarkably, as the man's authentic emotional state surfaced, Bella's behavior shifted. She stopped pacing, approached the man gently and stood quietly by his side. This change in Bella's behavior gave the man direct feedback that his newly aligned emotional state had a calming effect, reflecting the power of authenticity and emotional congruence.

These findings have profound implications for leadership coaching. They suggest leaders can work with horses to gain insight into their emotional alignment or misalignment. By engaging with horses, leaders can receive immediate and honest feedback on their non-verbal communication, helping to uncover and resolve internal discord. This process can lead to improved self-awareness, emotional intelligence and more authentic leadership practices that resonate with their human teams. This mirroring, wherein horses reflect their perceived emotional states, is vital to leadership development.

The Wisdom of Horses: Mirror Neurons and Non-Verbal Communication

Horses' capacity for non-verbal communication, deeply rooted in their evolutionary history and underpinned by mirror neurons, forms the backbone of their unique role in leadership coaching. This ability to communicate through non-verbal cues yields wisdom that can profoundly influence leadership coaching. The phenomenon of mirror neurons, specialized cells that activate when an individual performs an action or observes someone else doing the same, underscores horses' inborn sensitivity to human emotions and intentions. This neurological capacity enables horses to resonate with the subtlest shifts in human behavior, rendering them astute interpreters of incongruities between thoughts and feelings.

Mirror neurons, a neural phenomenon first discovered in macaque monkeys and subsequently observed in humans, have shed light on the cognitive mechanisms underpinning empathy and imitation. These specialized cells fire when an individual performs an action and when they witness someone else performing the same action. The significance of mirror neurons extends to horses, granting them the extraordinary ability to resonate with human emotions and intentions. The pioneering work of Rizzolatti and Sinigaglia (2010)[5] has provided compelling evidence of mirror neuron functionality in animals. These neurons enable humans and horses alike to understand and mimic the emotions and behaviors of others.

For example, one study by Rizzolatti and Sinigaglia demonstrated that certain brain areas in monkeys activated when they grabbed an object and watched another monkey make the same action, indicating the neurons' mirroring capability. Although it's more challenging to study mirror neurons directly in horses due to ethical and technical limitations, behavioral evidence strongly suggests that horses may possess a similar mirror neuron system. An example of how these findings translate to horse behavior can be seen in a study by Proops, McComb and colleagues (2013), which showed that horses could distinguish between attentive and inattentive human handlers and were more likely to approach an attentive person than an inattentive person. This suggests that horses are sensitive to human attentional states, likely through a mechanism akin to mirror neurons, allowing them to "mirror" or resonate with the emotional and attentional cues humans display.[6]

Though we share this ability, humans can often be deceived by cognitive bias and second-guessing their intuition. Reflect on when you picked up on someone's emotional state shift. Maybe you asked them about it. They assured you there wasn't a shift, you were reading into things too much. You may have believed them at the time, turning away from your intuition, only to find out later that you were right all along. At one time or another, most of us have lied about our emotional states, consciously or unconsciously. We know that sometimes it's simply easier to tell a "white lie" when asked how our day was than to admit to having a bad or stressful day. In the context of horses, this neurological capability allows them to detect even the subtlest incongruities between a person's thoughts and feelings, rendering them exceptionally sensitive interpreters of human emotional states. Unlike humans, they're not deterred by words and human bias in the way we often are. So, their observations can reveal authentic emotions and reactions that humans sometimes cannot pick up on.

Research-based findings affirm that horses respond to non-verbal cues and are adept at recognizing when a human's inner state mismatches their outward expression. By observing with their highly evolved senses and mirroring human emotional states, horses function as unbiased reflections, offering feedback untainted by human cognitive biases.

This study's results are particularly relevant to leadership coaching with horses. They support that horses can be a barometer for a leader's emotional congruence. For instance, when a leader feels anxious but attempts to project confidence, a horse may pick up on subtle physiological changes—like increased heart rate or muscle tension—inconsistent with the leader's outwardly calm demeanor. The horse might then become restless or hesitant, mirroring the leader's true emotional state rather than the façade they are presenting. Such findings have profound implications for the field of leadership development. They suggest that horses can be effective partners in helping leaders become more aware of their non-verbal communication and emotional authenticity. Leaders can improve their interpersonal interactions and create a more genuine connection with their teams by learning to align their inner feelings with their outer expressions.

Brain Development and Emotional Acumen

One major factor contributing to horses' ability to offer this incredible insight is their well-developed limbic system, a crucial part of their brain responsible for processing and regulating emotions. The limbic system is a complex set of structures located within the brain, often referred to as the "emotional brain" due to its significant role in processing and regulating emotions. It includes several key components, such as the amygdala, hippocampus, hypothalamus and various other interconnected regions. In horses, the limbic system functions in ways that are crucial for their survival as prey animals. It helps them process emotions and respond to environmental stimuli with appropriate behaviors. Each key component plays a significant part in keeping horses alive and safe:

- **Amygdala:** The amygdala detects threats and triggers the fight-or-flight response. When a horse senses danger, the amygdala activates this response, increasing heart rate and alertness, preparing the horse to either confront the threat or flee to safety.
- **Hippocampus:** The hippocampus plays a significant role in forming memories and learning from experiences, which is vital for horses to remember locations of food, water and territory boundaries. It also helps them recognize individuals within their herd and understand social hierarchies.
- **Hypothalamus:** The hypothalamus regulates the autonomic nervous system, influencing physiological responses to emotional states. For example, when a horse is calm and content, the hypothalamus helps maintain a steady heart rate and relaxed muscles. Conversely, when stressed or anxious, it can cause an increase in heart rate and muscle tension as part of the stress response.

Horses' limbic systems are highly evolved, enabling horses to accurately interpret and respond to a wide range of emotions. In the wild, their survival depended on swiftly recognizing potential threats and adapting to rapidly changing situations. Therefore, the development of their limbic system has been honed over millions of years of evolution, making them incredibly perceptive to emotional cues in their environment.

Humans also possess a limbic system responsible for processing emotions. However, what sets horses apart is the immediacy of their emotional responses. While humans can be trained to control or suppress emotional reactions consciously, horses react instinctively and swiftly. They excel in detecting incongruities in human behavior, meaning that horses are often quick to pick up on this disparity if a person is displaying one emotion while feeling another (a common human experience). Essentially, horses' emotional acumen, rooted in their well-developed limbic system, allows them to read human emotions remarkably well. This ability contributes to their role as powerful partners in coaching and therapy, as they can provide authentic and unbiased feedback based on their perception of human emotions, which is often more immediate and unfiltered than our own self-awareness. We can benefit from this information by observing what our equine partners are telling us, trusting their judgment and adjusting our approach based on the horse's insight.

Sight: The First Dimension of Perception

With their panoramic 350° vision, horses have evolved to constantly scan for potential threats or sudden movements. This visual acuity allows them to accurately read human body language cues signaling whether a situation is safe or potentially dangerous. For leaders, a horse's gaze and reactions provide candid feedback about their posture, energy and inner coherence between intention and impact. This capacity offers invaluable opportunities for interspecies communication and leadership development.

Studies by McGreevy et al. (2001) reveal that consistent, positive handling helps reduce stress in horses. Their research found that horses exhibited lower cortisol levels, heart rates and flight responses when trained using gentle, predictable routines vs. negative reinforcement or inconsistent handling.

McGreevy's team also measured how horses responded to different human postures and energies. Horses were willing to approach people exhibiting relaxed, confident body language, interpreted as non-threatening. Conversely, stressed or aggressive postures caused wariness and avoidance. Their research confirms horses accurately discern human emotional states through subtle physical cues.

This ability is likely owed to an evolutionary need to assess threats and social bonds within the herd. Horses in the wild depend on reading intention in others for survival. Studies reveal refined social cognition enables horses to relate to human emotional landscapes. This provides a gateway for interspecies understanding and communication.

For leaders, these findings emphasize the importance of congruence across verbal and non-verbal channels. Horses notice when expressions feel dissimilar to intention, indicating deception or inner discord. Consistently projecting confidence and positivity through body language and facial cues facilitates trust and cooperation, and horses demand authenticity, refusing to comply with mixed signals. By mirroring emotions accurately through their responses, horses provide experiential feedback about inner coherence and impact. Horses become unsettled if a leader claims calm but shows anxious body language. Their unease conveys the transparency of real intention beyond words. Leaders gain presence by aligning composure and intention and non-violent, non-verbal communion emerges.

Leading amid challenges requires managing distressing emotions so teams feel secure, focused energy from their leader. Horses will not cooperate with undisciplined reactivity, modeling the importance of regulation instead. Centering oneself in breath and bodily calm transmits composure, not chaos. Leadership presence strengthens. Relationships flourish when humans exhibit predictable routines and positive regard, communicating safety. Horses mirror these behaviors through willing participation and affection. They respond best to clear intentions centered on collective needs, teaching leaders that authority arises from service, not domination. Like horses, people crave *security* in leadership. Practicing non-violent communication with horses illuminates how leaders can attend to this universal need—fostering trust and cooperation through reliable care. Research confirms horses possess refined social cognition and non-verbal sensitivity. This allows them to accurately detect human emotions and intentions largely invisible to our conscious awareness. Horses see beneath words, titles and other trappings to the heart's truth. Their unmediated reactions provide a clear mirror into congruence and relational dynamics. Horses accelerate self-mastery by responding viscerally to qualities like authenticity, empathy and care in leadership. Their feedback exposes blind spots and cultivates emotional intelligence. Leaders gain presence by aligning intention with impact. They learn to regulate distress and exude calm confidence.

Relationships deepen as leaders apply horse teachings about establishing trust through reliable routines and compassionate regard. Teams thrive when given space for agency and growth. As in herds, authority arises through competence and service, not domination. At its core, non-violent communion with horses models leadership that fulfills a universal longing for security and shared purpose. Horses illuminate the path to self-awareness, inner coherence and care-centered influence. Their ancient wisdom helps leaders align words, intentions and impact in the service of teams and communities. Practicing horse teachings concentrates years of leadership growth into embodied integrity, unfolding step by step, breath by breath.

Furthermore, horses and humans perceive the world differently due to variations in their visual systems. As mentioned, horses have a broader field of vision than humans, with eyes positioned on the sides of their heads, enabling them to detect movement and potential threats from various angles. However, the frame rate or frames per second (fps) that horses can perceive is not explicitly documented in scientific research. Unlike some species, such as certain birds or insects, horses do not have specialized adaptations for high-speed vision. For humans, the frame rate at which smooth motion appears continuous is typically around 24 to 30 fps, so movies and videos are often filmed at these frame rates. Humans can perceive differences in frame rates above this threshold, such as the smoother motion seen at 60 fps compared to 30 fps, but there's a diminishing return in perceptual improvement.

With their different visual system, horses may have a higher or lower frame rate threshold for perceiving motion smoothly. While there isn't specific research on this topic, horses can likely perceive motion at rates similar to or slightly different from humans. However, this would depend on various factors, including their eyes' specific anatomy and functioning. The visual perception of horses, including their ability to perceive motion, is an important aspect to consider in equine-assisted coaching. While horses and humans share some similarities in visual processing, there are also distinct differences due to their unique evolutionary paths. As prey animals, horses have a visual system adapted for detecting motion across a wide field of view, which is crucial for their survival in the wild. This heightened sensitivity to movement can be leveraged in coaching to enhance the learning experience for leaders.

Understanding a horse's motion perception can inform coaching techniques involving non-verbal communication and body language. For instance, subtle changes in a coach's or participant's posture or gestures, which humans might overlook, could be readily detected by a horse. Leaders must be especially mindful of their movements and positioning during interactions with horses, as these animals may respond to cues that humans might not even consciously register. In coaching, horses' motion perception can become a valuable feedback mechanism. For example, the horse may perceive a leader's sudden or jerky movements as a sign of tension or nervousness, leading the horse to react with unease or alertness. Conversely, smooth and deliberate movements can convey confidence and calm, prompting a horse to respond similarly. By observing how horses react to their movements, leaders can gain insights into how their human team members might interpret their non-verbal behavior.

This knowledge can enhance coaching outcomes by encouraging leaders to develop greater self-awareness and control over their physical presence, which is often missed when considering how we interact with others. By refining their ability to communicate through movement and body language, leaders can improve their interactions with horses and within the professional environment, leading to better rapport, clearer communication and a more cohesive team dynamic.

Smell: The Olfactory Connection

Horses have a powerful sense of smell supported by nostrils that can flex to double in size for inhaling subtle scents. This allows them to detect pheromones, evaluate environmental signals and identify olfactory cues that may relate to human stress, fear or aggression. Their advanced odor-detection capacities add another layer of insight into human emotions. Horses possess a highly developed sense of smell beyond detecting mere scents. Research by Sabiniewicz et al. (2020) has illuminated their olfactory acumen, revealing their capacity to discern emotional states through scent cues. Horses can detect chemical signals in a person's scent, further underscoring their role as astute interpreters of human emotions and intentions. This research demonstrates that horses can distinguish between the body odors of fearful and happy humans, adding an intriguing layer to their non-verbal communication abilities. Thus, while humans primarily rely on verbal and visual cues for communication, horses incorporate olfactory information into their understanding of the world, providing additional insight into human emotional states.

Given that horses have a sensitive sense of smell, it's often recommended not to wear perfumes, colognes or scented lotions during coaching sessions with horses. The reason for this precaution is twofold. First, strong scents can overwhelm or distract a horse, possibly causing discomfort or anxiety. Just as a strong perfume might be overpowering for some humans, horses can react similarly to intense or unfamiliar scents. Second, strong perfumes can potentially bias a horse's reaction towards a person. Horses rely on their sense of smell to recognize individuals, and an unusual scent could mask the natural odors that a horse uses to identify someone, thereby affecting their response. For instance, a horse might not respond to a person as expected if their scent is masked by perfume, complicating the coaching process. In leadership coaching sessions, it is crucial to facilitate a clear and unbiased line of communication between the horse and the participant. Minimizing strong scents helps ensure that the horse's reactions are genuine and based on the participant's behavior and emotions, rather than being influenced by extraneous factors.

This attention to detail reinforces the importance of creating an environment that promotes authentic interactions, a valuable lesson in leadership beyond the coaching field. By considering the horse's comfort and sensory experience, leaders can learn to be more mindful and adaptive, ultimately fostering a more attentive and empathetic leadership style.

Hearing: The Auditory Awareness

Horses have a remarkably wide hearing range from 55 hertz (Hz) to 33 kilohertz (kHz) compared to the human range of 64 Hz to 23 kHz. Their large, mobile ears can swivel 180 degrees to hone in on and triangulate sounds with precision. They closely analyze qualities like voice tone, volume, tempo and intensity for information about human emotional states or intentions. Yelling or excessive loudness can stress horses by signaling aggression; calm, lower tones are more likely to reassure and establish trust. Horses' sensitive hearing extends beyond the range of human ears, allowing them to pick up on auditory cues that often escape human notice. Scientific studies, such as those conducted by Clayton et al. (2002),[7] have explored horses' auditory perception and ability to detect subtle vocal tone and intensity changes. One of the most remarkable aspects of horses' hearing is their capacity to detect sounds in the ultra-sonic range, a realm of frequencies beyond the reach of the human auditory system. It enables horses to perceive sounds at frequencies higher than 20,000 Hz, the upper limit of human hearing. Some studies have even indicated that horses can hear sounds with frequencies of up to 65,000 Hz or higher.

This heightened sense of hearing serves a crucial function in the horse-human relationship. Horses are exceptionally attuned to vocal tone and intensity changes in human speech. When a person communicates with a horse, even subtle variations in their vocal expressions, which might go unnoticed by other humans, are readily detected by the horse's ears. For example, if a human speaks with a soothing and calm tone, the horse may interpret this as a signal of safety and relaxation. Conversely, a human's nervousness or tension, reflected in vocal nuances, can trigger a heightened state of alertness or apprehension in the horse. This keen sense of hearing is particularly relevant in leadership coaching with horses. Participants often engage in non-verbal communication exercises in these contexts, by utilizing their non-verbal communication skills. Horses' ability to detect subtle changes in vocal tone and intensity can provide immediate feedback to participants about their emotional state and intentions, promoting self-awareness and authentic communication.

By observing how horses respond, we can also learn how to note these tone changes to understand better the people we're interacting with. Our hearing might not be as powerful as a horse's, but if we follow their lead in paying attention to the shifts in tone we *can* hear, we can become better at noticing and responding to these cues.

Touch: The Tactile Sensitivity

Horses' sensitive skin, aided by touch receptors in their manes and tails, allows them to detect subtle tactile cues like minute changes in pressure, vibration or texture. Mindful touch builds an emotional connection between humans and horses when delivered with care and awareness. Horses rely on tactile interactions for communication, bonding and as "windows" into human inner states. This sensitivity enables them to read emotions and intentions through physical contact, integral to their communication and interaction with the environment and members of the same species. Research by Hemmann et al. (2015)[8] highlights the importance of tactile interactions in horse-human relationships, demonstrating how horses respond to variations in touch pressure and quality. An example of how horses respond to variations in touch can be drawn from equine-assisted therapy sessions, where touch plays a critical role in communication between humans and horses.

Consider a session where a therapy horse named Willow interacts with a participant named Sarah. Sarah has been experiencing stress at work and is learning to manage her reactions through equine therapy. During a grooming exercise, Sarah begins to brush Willow gently, using long, soft strokes that relax both her and the horse. As Sarah becomes more comfortable, her touch becomes firmer, more confident and rhythmical. Willow responds to this change by leaning into the brush, signaling enjoyment and trust in Sarah's touch.

However, as Sarah's mind wanders to a recent stressful work event, her hands unconsciously grip the brush tighter, and her strokes become quicker and more erratic. Willow immediately feels the change in pressure and quality of touch, becoming tense and stepping away from Sarah. This reaction from Willow acts as a mirror to Sarah, indicating her internal state has shifted, even if she wasn't initially aware of it. This feedback moment allows Sarah to recognize the connection between her physical touch and emotional state. She takes a deep breath, releases the tension in her hands and returns to the calm, even strokes she started with. Feeling the change, Willow relaxes once again and steps closer, re-establishing the connection.

While humans use touch primarily for comforting or bonding, horses rely on it as a form of communication. Their heightened tactile sensitivity allows them to perceive subtle cues in human touch, enhancing their ability to mirror emotional states and provide feedback. There are many ways horses are better at sensing physical contact on a much broader scale than humans can.

- Horse Skin vs. Human Skin: Horses' skin is significantly more sensitive than human skin. This heightened sensitivity is attributed to a combination of factors, including the density of sensory receptors, the structure of the skin, and the presence of specialized sensory hairs called vibrissae.
- Vibrissae: Vibrissae, or "whiskers," on a horse's muzzle add another layer of tactile sensitivity. These whiskers are highly sensitive to touch and air movements, allowing horses to navigate their surroundings precisely.
- Tactile Discrimination: Horses excel in tactile discrimination, meaning they can discern fine details through touch. They use this ability extensively in social interactions with other horses, grooming and detecting subtle environmental changes.

- Importance in Communication: In horse-human interactions, horses rely on their sense of touch to communicate. They can detect minute variations in human touch, pressure and movements. This sensitivity enables them to respond to human cues and establishes trust and rapport. This explains why humans often guide horses through tactile means rather than relying mostly on commands, as we often do when training dogs.

Implications of the Horses' Tactile Sensitivity

- Gentle Handling: Horses' sensitive skin underscores the importance of gentle and respectful handling. A kind touch from humans has been found to positively influence horses' well-being and their willingness to engage in therapeutic activities.[9] Rough or aggressive handling can cause discomfort and stress to the horse. Humans have a history of using dominance and rough handling to control horses. However, enlightened with this deeper knowledge, we can benefit from the gifts horses have to offer us, gifts that aggression blocked us from accessing in previous generations.
- Communication in Leadership Coaching with Horses: As participants often engage in touch-based activities with horses, recognizing that horses can discern subtle tactile cues encourages participants to be mindful of their touch and its impact on the horse. For example, grooming can be used to promote stress reduction. Research has shown that grooming is a fundamental aspect of equine social behavior and reduces stress in horses.[10] Grooming sessions involving touch and rhythmic movements promote relaxation by stimulating the release of endorphins, which are natural mood enhancers for humans and horses.
- Trust and Bonding: Developing trust and a strong bond between humans and horses relies on considerate tactile interactions. Knowing that horses can perceive nuanced touches fosters a deeper connection between the two species.

Touch has a profound impact on human well-being. Human-to-human touch triggers the release of oxytocin, often called the "*love hormone*" or "*bonding hormone.*" Oxytocin is associated with feelings of trust, empathy and relaxation. This hormone also contributes to reducing stress and anxiety. It is known that physical touch, such as hugging or holding hands, leads to increased oxytocin release in humans. This hormonal response promotes relaxation and a sense of emotional connection.[11]

Furthermore, the practice of mindfulness often incorporates touch as a grounding technique. A study by Kerr et al. (2011) explored the effects of mindful touch on stress reduction. Participants who engaged in mindful touch exercises reported reduced stress levels and increased feelings of relaxation and well-being.[12] Being aware of the useful impacts of touch allows us to better bond with horses and each other, offering a tool for managing our stress levels, which is essential for good leadership. When humans engage in mindful touch with horses, such as grooming or massage, they become attuned to the present moment. This tactile connection fosters a sense of mindfulness, where individuals focus on the sensations and interactions at hand, temporarily setting aside worries and distractions.

The reciprocal nature of touch-based interactions with horses reinforces the sense of trust, empathy and relaxation. Horses respond positively to gentle and mindful touch, creating a symbiotic relationship that benefits both species.

Taste: A Secondary Sense

Taste and smell form a critical part of a horse's sensory perception and play an important role in their interaction with the environment. While taste is a secondary sense for horses in the context of leadership coaching, it remains integral to their holistic sensory experience. Horses use their sense of taste in conjunction with smell to decide what to eat, which objects to explore and how to make sense of the environment around them.

Establishing Trust and Building Rapport with Horses

Trust and rapport are the cornerstones upon which meaningful progress is built in leadership coaching with horses. These foundational elements are vital in human-client relationships or partnerships with our equine companions.[13] As we delve deeper into this chapter, we'll discover trust-building's pivotal role in various dimensions of coaching and human interaction and how it extends far beyond mere mechanical techniques.

To cultivate a profound connection with a horse, it's imperative to understand their nature, unique cues and the essence of non-verbal communication.[14] This involves embodying respect, empathy and effective communication characteristics that resonate deeply with horses and humans alike. Creating an environment conducive to safe and productive coaching sessions with horses hinges on establishing trust between humans and these magnificent creatures. This bond, rooted in a nuanced comprehension of equine body language, demands an approach that places respect at the forefront. It also involves nurturing mutual understanding where the horse becomes a partner and collaborator. Astonishingly, the techniques used to build rapport with our equine partners often parallel those employed in leadership contexts. Mastering these skills enhances our ability to work effectively with horses and translates seamlessly into fostering productive relationships and communication within human teams.

Building Trust and Safety in Equine-Assisted Coaching

Creating a secure environment grounded in mutual trust and respect is essential for productive leadership coaching with horses. As prey animals, horses are hardwired to detect potential threats. They read human intention through subtle cues like body language, vocal tone and energy. Horses reciprocate calm, confident leadership with willingness and cooperation. But anxiety or ambiguity elicits wariness. This makes establishing psychological safety paramount. When approaching horses, leaders must align composure with benevolent purpose. Incongruities signal deception, triggering a horse's flight response. Only with trusted humans do horses relax their hypervigilance. They cooperate fully when leaders radiate strength of purpose through tranquil presence. This model for leaders shows how authentic alignment—between inner state and outer expression—unlocks influence through trust.

Imagine Alex, an executive skeptical of equine coaching. In his first session, self-doubt permeates his tentative cues despite acting confident. Sensing discordance, his horse partner Luna grows distracted, ignoring Alex's directions. Drawing on her expertise, the coach guides Alex to pause and refocus inwardly. Centering himself on purpose, Alex reapproaches Luna with resolute calm. As Alex's confidence aligns internally and externally, Luna mirrors his composure. She begins following Alex's clear guidance, restoring their harmonious partnership.

This vignette demonstrates the impact of leader coherence on securing horses' engagement. Luna's initial resistance reflected Alex's inner ambivalence leaking through façades of control. Only when Alex projects certainty grounded in authentic self-belief does Luna comply. This experiential lesson magnifies for Alex how teams respond to total integrity of leadership. Equine specialists design sessions to reveal and strengthen this integrity. Activities focus on clear communication, emotional regulation and physical awareness—skills transferable to human leadership. Coaches then guide reflection on how horse interactions illuminate development areas, and participants integrate insights about aligning confidence and care to motivate others.

Foundational knowledge of horse psychology allows coaches to facilitate effectively. Understanding herd dynamics and roles provides perspective on team leadership. Horses perform distinct functions to support group welfare, paralleling workplace collaboration. There are lessons here about aligning talent and authority. Like people, each horse also has a unique personality shaping relational needs; therefore, coaches must empathize and adapt approaches to suit different horses' temperaments. They demonstrate leading responsively vs. rigidly. Even simple acts, such as grooming, offer teachings about being fully present with colleagues' needs and tendencies.

Safety is also woven into the space itself. Coaching takes place in enclosed arenas or pastures where horses feel secure. Inviting leaders into this domain requires vigilance. Coaches position themselves between horse and human if needed and they watch for stress in either participant, adjusting the process accordingly. Horses are never forced beyond their comfort zone and psychological safety remains a priority. Demonstrating this care builds leaders' trust in the process. Feeling safe to explore new experiences unleashes transformational growth. Coaches hold space for authenticity to emerge through these experiences and guided reflection. Over time, leaders shed protective pretenses and relate to horses from wholeness and the arena becomes a field of possibility for enacting one's highest purpose.

These lessons translate into more empowering leadership across contexts. Leaders begin replacing fear-based manipulation with care-centered influence, grounded in accountability. They listen more empathetically, adapting to unique needs. Teams feel valued for their contributions and empowered to excel. Fundamentally, horses demand secure environments, allowing vulnerability. They invite leaders to extend that compassion to everyone. When people feel safe to bring their full, authentic selves to work, they invest more and produce quality outcomes. They also serve the organization's purpose with integrity.

Establishing psychological safety and trust is essential to transformative leadership coaching with horses. Skilled facilitation considers both human and horse needs, guiding purposeful engagement and reflection. Leaders are challenged to align inner and outer authority before horses cooperate. This experiential lesson sticks with the leader outside the arena, prompting the integration of authentic, care-based relating with colleagues. Safe coaching spaces permit deeper self-discovery. Horses unlock learning by first nurturing environments where the human spirit feels protected, yet inspired to expand. Their sensitivity compels leaders to show up authentically and lead humanely. Teams thrive when people feel seen, valued and secure enough to contribute freely. In the end, horses themselves model unconditional positive regard and vulnerable courage, and continue to invite connection when we respectfully approach them. They epitomize resilient trust and cooperation guided by care. May we honor and emulate their noble example in leadership and life.

Ethical Considerations in Coaching with Horses

The privilege of partnering with horses in coaching carries profound ethical responsibilities. Beyond upholding basic welfare, we must approach horses with reverence for their sentience and autonomy. They deserve no less in exchange for their teachings.

Likewise, we owe participants psychological safety during deep personal explorations. Relating skillfully and ethically with horses requires understanding their natures and needs. Horses are highly social herd animals. Their survival depends on tight-knit groups with hierarchical bonds, and each member fills a role supporting collective thriving, not unlike human teams. Horses also have defined territories in the wild. Entering a horse's space demands respect. They experience stress when boundaries get violated, just as people do. Their sensitivity compels compassion. As prey, horses excel at reading human intention through body language and energy. They reflect back our innermost emotional states, often beyond conscious awareness. This makes horses exceptionally responsive partners for modeling leadership qualities like mindfulness, empathy and service. But it also renders them vulnerable to human toxicity. Unresolved anger or ego can fracture the human-horse connection in seconds. Thus, an ethical foundation for horse coaching begins with leaders' commitment to personal growth. Doing our inner work allows horses to approach in trust and mutual understanding. The quality of our relationship flows from internal integrity. With mindset aligned, we can then structurally uphold horses' well-being. Some key areas include:

- Physical welfare: Providing horses with top-quality nutrition, veterinary care, shelter and environments suited to their needs. This sustains their health and longevity as coaching partners.
- Training approach: Using positive reinforcement, not punishment or force. Skilled coaches tap inherent horse motivations and channel them toward voluntary participation.
- Workload balance: Limiting horses' coaching hours and intensities. Regular breaks in their schedules reduce burnout. Work aligns with each horse's preferences and stamina.
- Autonomy and consent: Letting horses determine their comfort with activities and participants. Pushing past expressed boundaries damages trust and psychological safety.
- Relational skill-building: Deepening coaches' abilities to read subtle horse cues around fatigue, discomfort, engagement and stress. This nuanced awareness allows for continually improving horse care.
- Ongoing education: Staying current on advancing best practices in horse welfare science and training philosophy. Lifelong learning fine-tunes the human role in partnership.
- Resource investment: Providing high-caliber facilities, trainers, veterinary care and herd environments. Compromising here corrodes ethically centered coaching.
- Gratitude and reverence: Regarding horses as sacred teachers despite our history of domination. They keep offering wisdom, asking little in return. Our respect must match this extraordinary gift.

Essentially, horses provide a mirror into how we lead. The more we cultivate presence and care for their well-being, the more horses reveal our human potential. Their service compels reciprocity through developing leadership as an ethic of empowerment, not control.

Upholding Participant Psychological Safety

As we covenant to honor horse welfare, coaches owe participants an environment allowing deep personal exploration. Vulnerability requires psychological safety. We can earn participants' trust through:

- Establishing confidentiality: No shared content or insights get disclosed outside sessions. Participants understand materials are kept secure.
- Informed consent: Review activities in advance and ensure participants never feel pressured to exceed their comfort zones. Patience is shown with their boundaries.
- Embodying care: Holding a safe space with warmth and compassion. Allowing emotions to surface and be felt without judgment. Physical contact only occurs with consent.
- Active listening: Giving undivided attention to participants and suspending assumptions. Reflective listening affirms understanding. Open-ended questions draw insights out gently.
- Encouraging supportively: Validating courage and providing specific positive feedback on progress. Avoiding negativity.
- Permission for imperfection: Normalizing stumbles as universal aspects of growth. Neither coaches nor horses expect perfection. Celebrating efforts, not outcomes.
- Accessibility: Accommodating disabilities and diverse backgrounds graciously. Adapting activities to enable all willing participants.
- Follow-up care: Checking on participants' integration process after intensive sessions. Avoiding abrupt detachment. Offering further resources as desired.

When leaders feel safe to explore their deepest waters around purpose and relationships, clarity follows. By courageously examining where they stand today, participants then have the honesty and self-compassion to take the next step forward. The coach's goal is to create conditions where honesty can emerge through experiential discovery and integration. Holding this safe space honors the vulnerabilities participants reveal in service to their higher calling.

Walking the Talk: Aligning Coaching Ethics and Practice

There are many steps involved in offering ethical, results-based coaching to leaders and their equine partners:

- Educating ourselves on evidence-based horse welfare and relational wisdom; this breaks cycles of ignorance.
- Carefully screening prospective horses and participants for mutual suitability; avoid forcing mismatched companions.

- Role modeling vulnerability and mutual care through kind, clear intentions relating with horses and humans; this sets a positive path.
- Intervening immediately when safety—physical or emotional—gets compromised. Allowing even micro-abuses normalizes them, and that cannot be allowed to happen.
- Celebrating horses' efforts using motivators meaningful to them, such as praise, scratches and rest. Punishers like yelling only degrade the horse-human bond.
- Admitting knowledge gaps with humility and pursuing continuing education. No one ever *"arrives"* perfectly wise.
- Keeping horse work varied, stimulating their minds and bodies. Boredom taxes their spirit. Enrichment nurtures it.
- Evaluating facilities and resource allocations from the horse's perspective. *Are their fundamental needs met joyfully?* Considering horses' dignity first when dilemmas arise. Their vulnerability earns extra advocacy.
- Infusing reverence and gratitude into all we do. This mindset elevates standards and inspires service.

To develop ethical leadership in others, we must nurture that seed within ourselves. Coaching, grounded in respect, begets more enlightened relating across contexts. The state of our inner world surfaces in the outer world through subtle, energetic expressions. Horses naturally read and respond to this unconscious integrity. By walking our truth fully, we pass the torch through modeling vs. mandate.

The Path Ahead: Next Steps in Advancing Equine Coaching Ethics

While ethical coaching rests on timeless principles, applying them well requires updating approaches as research and public sensibilities evolve. Some emerging frontiers include:

- Independent horse welfare certification programs with defined standards, assessments and audits
- Increased emphasis on understanding the psychology and social dynamics of horses within herds
- Nuanced metrics to evaluate horse stress levels during human activities
- Advances in positive reinforcement training to deepen willing horse participation
- Growing public concern about horse treatment, compelling ever-higher standards
- Pressure for facilities education, accreditation and reporting transparency
- Formal ethical training requirements for professionals seeking equine coaching credentials

- Expanding veterinary knowledge of horse health, optimizing longevity and coaching capacity
- Technologies allowing detailed monitoring of biometrics signaling horse comfort and fatigue
- Greater inclusivity, access and support for diverse coaching participants

The path ahead promises continued evolution in how humanity partners with these magnificent creatures. As stewards of that relationship, coaches carry immense responsibility. Coaches must walk this road with wisdom earned from horses—the greatest guides on the journey to ethical leadership and service.

Notes

1 Kahneman, D. (2011). *Thinking, fast and slow.* Farrar, Straus and Giroux.
2 Bachi, K. (2013). Equine-facilitated psychotherapy: The gap between practice and knowledge. *Society & Animals,* 20(4), 364–380.
3 Smith, A. V., Proops, L., Grounds, K., Wathan, J., & McComb, K. (2016). Functionally relevant responses to human facial expressions of emotion in the domestic horse. *Biology Letters,* 12(2). https://doi.org/10.1098/rsbl.2015.0907.
4 Rizzolatti, G., & Sinigaglia, C. (2016). The mirror mechanism: A basic principle of brain function. *Nature Reviews Neuroscience,* 17(12), 757–765.
5 Rizzolatti, G., & Sinigaglia, C. (2010). The functional role of the parieto-frontal mirror circuit: Interpretations and misinterpretations. *Nature Reviews Neuroscience,* 11(4), 264–274. Proops, L., & McComb, K. (2013). Attributing attention: The use of human-given cues by domestic horses (*Equus caballus*). *Animal Cognition,* 16(2), 197–205.
6 Proops, L., & McComb, K. (2013). Attributing attention: The use of human-given cues by domestic horses (*Equus caballus*). *Animal Cognition,* 16(2), 197–205.
7 Clayton, H. M., & Singleton, W. H. (2002). Ethogram of behaviours observed in horses during trailer loading. *Equine Veterinary Journal,* 34(S34), 140–143.
8 Hemmann, K., & Bockisch, F. J. (2015). The skin's role in horse-human tactile communication. *Applied Animal Behaviour Science,* 162, 69–76.
9 Bachi, K., Terkel, J., & Teichman, M. (2012). Equine reactions to a human grooming approach. *Journal of Veterinary Behavior,* 7(4), 237–243.
10 Hausberger, M., Roche, H., Henry, S., & Visser, E. K. (2008). A review of the human–horse relationship. *Applied Animal Behaviour Science,* 109(1), 1–24.
11 Holt-Lunstad, J., Birmingham, W. A., & Light, K. C. (2008). Influence of a "warm touch" support enhancement intervention among married couples on ambulatory blood pressure, oxytocin, alpha amylase, and cortisol. *Psychosomatic Medicine,* 70(9), 976–985.
12 Kerr, C. E., Sacchet, M. D., Lazar, S. W., Moore, C. I., & Jones, S. R. (2011). Mindfulness starts with the body: Somatosensory attention and top-down modulation of cortical alpha rhythms in mindfulness meditation. *Frontiers in Human Neuroscience,* 5, 1–15.
13 King, C. E., & Hemsworth, P. H. (2020). Horse-human interactions and the effect on the behaviour and welfare of horses. *Applied Animal Behaviour Science,* 234, 105168.
14 Ponzo, V., Kubiak, T., & Kossowska, M. (2018). Neuroscience of communication—Part 2: Mimicry and "theory of mind." *Journal of Education, Culture and Society,* 1(2), 113–124.

Chapter 2

Integrating Biofeedback in Coaching

Exploring Biofeedback

Biofeedback represents a powerful integration of science and self-awareness, allowing individuals to gain real insight into their physiological responses. By examining the origins and evolution of biofeedback technology and key research studies, we can better understand its core principles and intrinsic value within coaching and leadership development. The origins of biofeedback can be traced back to the groundbreaking work of Dr. Neal E. Miller in the 1960s.[1] A distinguished American psychologist, Dr. Miller, conducted important experiments with animals, especially rats, demonstrating that they could be trained to gain conscious control over physiological processes like heart rate and blood pressure. This led to the revolutionary suggestion that humans, too, might be capable of exerting voluntary control over their bodily functions.

Dr. Miller's work laid the foundation for the biofeedback field to blossom over the ensuing decades. In the 1970s, Dr. Elmer Green and his wife Alyce[2] conducted an influential study with Tibetan Buddhist monks who had undergone extensive training in meditation and mindfulness. Using biofeedback technology to monitor the monks' heart rate, body temperature and brain waves, they found that monks could exert remarkable voluntary control over these bodily functions during meditation. This provided concrete evidence of their ability to enter states of relaxation and willfully alter their physiology.

After its beginnings in the 1960s and 70s, biofeedback continued to gain momentum through the following decades. By the 1980s and 90s, a new generation of simpler and more accessible biofeedback devices emerged, alongside a growing body of clinical research demonstrating its efficacy for treating conditions like chronic pain, hypertension and migraine headaches. This fueled wider adoption in therapeutic contexts. Today, consumer-grade wearable devices have brought personalized biofeedback to millions, providing real-time data on metrics like heart rate variability (HRV) and sleep patterns. As biofeedback technology becomes further democratized, its self-

DOI: 10.4324/9781032683843-3

awareness, personal development and peak performance applications will expand exponentially across diverse fields.

Biofeedback has particularly powerful applications when integrated thoughtfully into coaching and leadership development. During coaching sessions, biofeedback metrics can reveal how clients physiologically respond to various inquiry, reflection and perspective-sharing forms. This allows coaches to better align interventions based on observed arousal and stress patterns. For clients, reviewing biofeedback data from coaching sessions helps anchor insights and strengthen self-awareness of emotional triggers and reactions. Over time, this enhances metacognition and conscious choice over automatic reactive patterns. Similarly, leaders can leverage biofeedback while delivering speeches or during high-pressure interactions to recognize unproductive stress responses and purposefully self-regulate. Thus, biofeedback unlocks invaluable mind-body insights for growth and mastery, whether used during formal coaching or for self-directed learning.

Biofeedback can be understood as a process enabling real-time monitoring of bodily functions like heart rate, breathing, muscle tension, skin temperature and brain waves. This bridges the conscious and subconscious minds, surfacing subtle physiological cues that often go unnoticed. For instance, biofeedback can reveal the racing heart, sweaty palms and intrusive thoughts accompanying public-speaking anxiety. This self-awareness allows individuals to recognize how anxiety manifests physically, understand its impacts, and potentially learn to mitigate unhelpful responses through practice. Lauri Nummenmaa's seminal research on "Bodily Maps of Emotions" also demonstrates the importance of physical and non-verbal cues in social contexts. Nummenmaa showed how basic emotions manifest in the body (Figure 2.1, below). The resulting visual representations reveal emotion-specific patterns of affected areas. For instance, anxiety largely impacts the upper chest, while depression centers around the head, and fear activates the hands and feet. This provides tangible guides for recognizing non-verbal cues based on physiological signals.

Integrating biofeedback technology into coaching can help leaders develop deeper body awareness and emotional intelligence. For instance, HRV biofeedback enables tracking arousal levels during interactions to understand stress responses. Biofeedback-guided breathing and mindfulness exercises also facilitate relaxation. This empowers leaders to perceive their bodily states better, regulate destructive responses and embody constructive leadership presence.

Biofeedback offers a window into the rich dynamics of our physiological functioning. While its origins trace back more than 50 years, biofeedback science continues to evolve rapidly. When woven skillfully into coaching and leader development, Biofeedback provides data-driven pathways for self-discovery, emotional mastery and empowering transformation. The mind-body insights it unveils are indispensable for coaches and leaders progressing their developmental journeys.

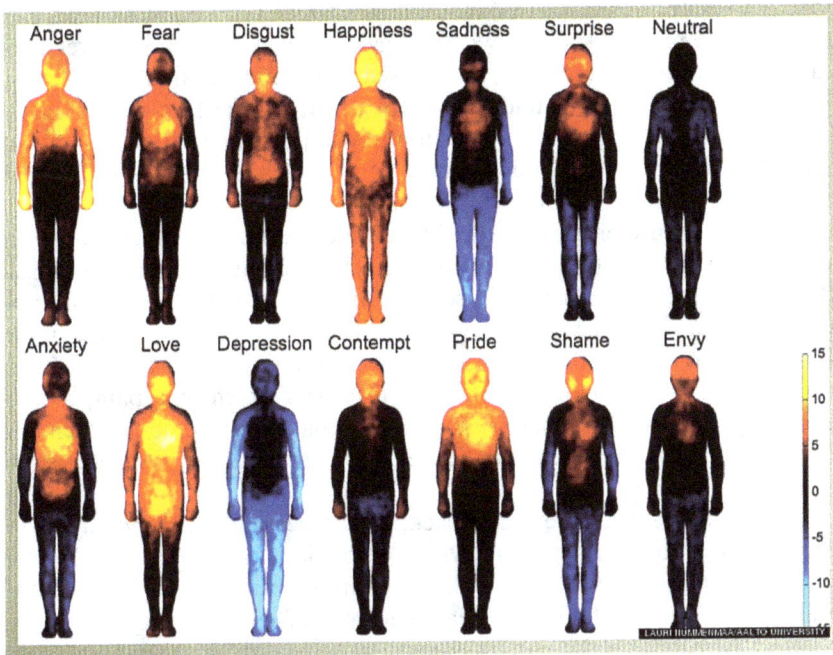

Figure 2.1 Bodily topography of basic (*Upper*) and non-basic (*Lower*) emotions associated with words. The body maps show regions whose activation increased (warm colors) or decreased (cool colors) when feeling each emotion. (P < 0.05 FDR corrected; t > 1.94). The colorbar indicates the t-statistic range

Source: Bodily maps of emotions, Lauri Nummenmaa (lauri.nummenmaa@aalto.fi), Enrico Glerean, Riitta Hari (lauri.nummenmaa@aalto.fi), and Jari K. Hietanen. https://doi.org/10.1073/pnas.1321664111.

The How Behind the What

As a therapeutic technique, biofeedback offers a granular view of the body's physiological functions, providing a unique interface for self-regulation and psychological well-being. It utilizes sophisticated equipment and sensors to capture real-time data on various physiological responses, thus facilitating a feedback loop where individuals can learn to influence their autonomic functions. Central to biofeedback is the measurement of parameters such as HRV, skin conductance (also known as galvanic skin response, or GSR), electromyography (EMG), electroencephalography (EEG), skin temperature and respiration rate. Each of these metrics offers insight into the functioning of different aspects of the autonomic nervous system and serves as a cornerstone for biofeedback training modalities.

HRV, in particular, measures the time variance between consecutive heartbeats and reflects autonomic nervous system activity. It is a well-regarded index for assessing physiological resilience and flexibility and an individual's capacity to adapt to stress. HRV biofeedback, which often employs heart rate monitors, is a method through which individuals can gain control over their heart rate patterns, thus affecting stress reduction and emotional regulation. The importance of HRV is underscored by research from Hye-Geum Kim et al. (2018), [3] who explored its connection to emotional regulation, suggesting that HRV indicates the body's capacity to manage psychological stress effectively.

Skin conductance biofeedback and EMG biofeedback are other modalities that enable the regulation of the sympathetic nervous system and muscle activity, respectively. While GSR sensors measure the skin's electrical conductance as an indicator of stress, EMG sensors monitor muscle activity to aid in relaxation and tension release. These modalities are particularly beneficial for individuals with stress-related disorders or chronic pain, as evidenced by Jacobson's[4] Progressive Muscle Relaxation method, which has been empirically validated for its efficacy in reducing somatic stress responses.

EEG biofeedback, or neurofeedback, is another advanced modality that harnesses the brain's electrical activity to modulate cognitive states. It is an area of growing interest, with applications in attention disorders, cognitive enhancement and mental health treatment. Neurofeedback trains individuals to alter their brainwave patterns—such as alpha, beta, theta and delta waves—through direct feedback, promoting mental states conducive to focus or relaxation. Its effectiveness is supported by a robust body of research, including studies that have demonstrated its potential in improving symptoms of ADHD and anxiety disorders.

Temperature and respiration biofeedback round out the biofeedback modalities, offering methods for individuals to regulate their thermal and respiratory responses. These techniques have been associated with relaxation training and stress management, with evidence supporting their use in clinical settings to ameliorate conditions like hypertension and respiratory ailments.

The efficacy of biofeedback is not just anecdotal—it is well-documented in scientific literature. A wealth of studies have established biofeedback as a valid technique for stress reduction, emotional regulation and cognitive performance optimization. For instance, HRV biofeedback has been shown to contribute to reduced stress levels and improved emotional health, providing a non-pharmacological avenue for managing anxiety and stress-related disorders.[5] Such findings reinforce the value of biofeedback as a potent tool in the arsenal of psychological interventions.

Applications of Biofeedback in Leadership Development

Biofeedback, specifically within leadership development, signifies an innovative and multidimensional approach to cultivating the core capabilities integral to effective leadership. This integration represents a progressive shift towards more holistic development strategies emphasizing the intricate interrelation between mind and body. By furnishing leaders with real-time insights into their physiological states, biofeedback opens a portal into a deeper understanding of the somatic manifestations of stress and emotion. This understanding is invaluable for enhancing self-awareness, emotional intelligence and resilience.

At its essence, the notion of biofeedback in leadership involves leveraging physiological signals as a mirror for illuminating internal states. Among the various metrics that can be monitored, HRV has risen to prominence as a significant indicator, owing to its correlation with cardiac vagal tone—a measure of the body's capacity to engage regulatory systems and maintain equilibrium in the face of external challenges (Laborde, Mosley & Thayer, 2017).[6] As Laborde et al. explicate, HRV signifies a marker of such self-regulatory potential, underscoring its importance for adaptive leadership. In the fast-paced and frequently unpredictable environments navigated by contemporary leaders, the capability to uphold composure, sustain clarity of thought and execute sound decision-making under intense pressure is greatly augmented by a finely tuned cardiac vagal tone.

The pioneering work undertaken by the HeartMath[7] Institute further highlights the significance of heart-centered biofeedback in leadership development contexts. Their extensive corpus of research explores the psychophysiological coherence model, where a high degree of synchronization among various bodily systems—notably between the heart and brain—is linked with optimal functioning. Leaders trained to induce and preserve psychophysiological coherence can more effectively regulate stress, enhance cognitive faculties and sustain emotional stability. The HeartMath Institute's techniques, frequently involving HRV biofeedback, have engendered such coherent states, empowering leaders to operate from a place of balance and composure. Yet this coherence represents not merely a fixed state to be attained, but a dynamic and adaptive quality that adroit leaders can cultivate and deploy strategically. For instance, the capacity to enter a coherent state during complex decision-making processes or high-stakes negotiations endows leaders with a competitive advantage, allowing them to respond thoughtfully rather than react impulsively, listen deeply with presence and connect genuinely with others.

Incorporating sophisticated technology within biofeedback systems unveils new frontiers in personalized coaching and self-regulation modalities. AI-powered analytics enable the processing of voluminous quantities of physiological data in real-time, granting leaders enhanced clarity into their emotional states and stress levels. Wearable biofeedback devices—like smartwatches and specialized wearables—can continuously monitor physiological input, supplying leaders with instant insights into heart rate, stress levels and other vital metrics. This level of accessibility renders these pieces of technology potentially transformative tools for leadership development. Additionally, machine learning algorithms are indispensable for unraveling subtle patterns in biofeedback information. These algorithms can analyze multifaceted datasets—such as brainwave patterns—to identify nuanced shifts and predict emotional triggers, aiding leaders in devising developmental strategies. The precision, personalization and predictive potential of these technologies, paired with safeguarding the privacy and security of sensitive data, herald a new era in leadership development.

The implications of biofeedback for leadership extend beyond personal mastery; they ripple into influencing and reinventing organizational culture. Leaders who actively implement biofeedback and hone these competencies will inevitably model behaviors and mindsets that engender a healthier, more resilient workforce. They become champions of a workplace ecology that cherishes mindfulness, emotional intelligence and stress management, not merely as abstract ideals but as concrete, quantifiable and learnable skills.

As technology advances swiftly, the potential for more sophisticated biofeedback applications in leadership development escalates correspondingly. However, ensuring these technologies remain understandable, usable and widely accessible for leaders across backgrounds remains an ongoing challenge. This vision explores the pathways for developing more self-aware, emotionally attuned leaders through the ingenious integration of biofeedback systems and technology. While the origins of biofeedback can be traced back more than 50 years, the science continues to evolve exponentially. A new generation of consumer-friendly wearable devices has now placed personalized biofeedback into the hands of millions. As HRV monitoring becomes further democratized through consumer-wearable technology, its self-knowledge, personal growth and professional development applications will rapidly expand across diverse fields.

For instance, biofeedback metrics can grant valuable insights into clients' stress patterns and emotional triggers in coaching. Reviewing HRV data from coaching sessions helps anchor insights and strengthen self-awareness around reactions and responses. Over time, this builds metacognition and conscious choice over habitual reactive tendencies. Leaders can similarly leverage biofeedback during speeches or high-pressure interactions to recognize unproductive stress reactions and purposefully self-regulate. Thus, whether employed in structured coaching or independent practice, biofeedback unlocks invaluable mind-body insights for actualization and mastery.

Integrating biofeedback and coaching can also be powerfully catalyzed through online delivery methods. Virtual coaching and remote biofeedback monitoring enable coaches to guide clients through self-regulation techniques and emotional-intelligence growth from anywhere. As virtual coaching increases in prevalence, these blended models—granting coaches real-time access to clients' physiological data—can significantly enhance attunement and impact. However, while propelled by rapid innovation, integrating biofeedback into leadership development contexts still raises complex ethical challenges. As data privacy and security concerns intensify, establishing robust safeguards to protect individuals' sensitive information remains critically important, demanding thoughtful protocols and policies. There is also a risk of over-reliance on biofeedback metrics without a nuanced interpretation of what underlies the data. Navigating these complexities requires ethical care from coaches and practitioners leveraging biofeedback to avoid mechanistic applications.

At its heart, biofeedback provides a window into our dynamic physiology and psychology that reveals as much about our common humanity as it does our uniqueness. Although its technical origins trace back decades, biofeedback's capacity for catalyzing human flourishing through self-knowledge and actualization has only begun to be explored.

Accessibility and Inclusivity of Biofeedback

The democratization of biofeedback technology is a testament to the advancements in accessibility and user-friendliness in the tools available for personal health and performance monitoring. One of the standout examples in this evolution is the application HRV4Training,[8] which leverages the smartphone camera to measure HRV. This app allows users to assess their HRV without needing additional hardware. It is an excellent option for individuals interested in personal health tracking or for coaches incorporating biofeedback into their practice.

HRV4Training uses the phone's camera to detect pulse rate by capturing subtle changes in the color of the fingertip, which is synchronous with the heartbeat. This data then calculates HRV as a reliable marker of autonomic nervous system activity and an individual's stress and recovery status. Over time, by consistently measuring HRV, the application can provide insights into the user's physiological responses to stress, exercise and relaxation. For leadership coaching, such insights can be particularly valuable; they can help determine if a leader is over-stressed or not recovering adequately, thus impairing decision-making and emotional regulation. In parallel, wearable watches with sensors that measure blood oxygenation levels, another metric often included in wearable devices, can inform users about breathing patterns and overall cardiovascular health. This can be particularly insightful during physical or mentally taxing segments of leadership coaching, ensuring the leader is engaged and physiologically capable of sustaining focus and energy.

The confluence of such technologies in leadership coaching underscores a holistic approach to development that recognizes the interplay between physiological well-being and effective leadership. It allows for a nuanced understanding of how different facets of leadership—from communication to crisis management—affect a leader's physical state, which can impact their behavior and decision-making.

Incorporating HRV4Training and similar applications into leadership coaching embraces a longitudinal approach, recognizing that the true value of HRV lies in observing trends over time rather than isolated measurements. Over a prolonged period, leaders can use such applications to establish a baseline HRV level and then record their HRV under various conditions throughout their leadership journey. This consistent monitoring can reveal how leadership tasks, decision-making processes and interpersonal interactions influence their autonomic nervous system.

For example, a leader might take daily HRV measurements first thing in the morning, creating a personal database of how their stress and recovery levels fluctuate in relation to their professional activities. Over weeks or months, patterns may emerge, showing how specific leadership challenges correlate with changes in HRV. Coaches can then review this data with the leaders, helping them to identify which activities are associated with stress or recovery. This insight enables them to adopt targeted strategies for managing their physiological response to certain leadership scenarios. The analogy to athletic training is apt when considering a leader's workday as a series of performance periods akin to a training regimen. Just as athletes use bio-feedback to understand when to push their limits and when to recover, leaders can use wearable devices that measure HRV, blood oxygenation and other biometrics to gauge their performance readiness and recovery needs. These wearables can provide a detailed picture of when a leader is most alert and focused, when they might need to schedule restful periods or when they are best suited for high-stakes tasks.

By treating a workday like a training session, leaders can learn to optimize their schedules according to their physiological states. For instance, if a wearable device indicates that blood oxygenation levels and HRV are optimal, the leader might tackle the most demanding tasks of the day during this peak performance window. Conversely, if the device shows signs of physiological stress or reduced recovery, the leader might engage in restorative activities, such as deep-breathing exercises or a brief walk, to facilitate a return to a more balanced state. Through consistent application and interpretation of biofeedback data, leaders can improve their immediate response to stress and develop long-term strategies for enhancing resilience and performance. This scientifically informed approach fosters a culture of self-awareness and proactive well-being management within the leadership practice.

Integrating Biofeedback with Coaching with Horses

Integrating biofeedback into coaching sessions with horses represents a groundbreaking approach that marries the therapeutic power of equine-assisted activities with the precision of physiological measurement. With their remarkable sensitivity to human emotional states, horses provide a dynamic and responsive context for individuals to explore and develop self-awareness and leadership abilities. This innovative method is further bolstered by research that examines HRV in horses engaged in such activities.

The study conducted by Gehrke, Baldwin and Schiltz (2011)[9] investigated the HRV in horses during equine-assisted activities, offering compelling insights into the mutual physiological engagement between horses and humans. It showed that humans experience changes in their HRV during interactions with horses and exhibit alterations in their HRV, suggesting a bidirectional influence and a shared emotional and physiological connection. In leadership development, the implications of this research are profound. By integrating HRV biofeedback in equine-assisted coaching sessions, leaders gain access to an immediate and authentic gauge of their internal state as mirrored by the horse. This biofeedback loop allows for a deeper exploration into the leader's emotional processing and stress management strategies, facilitating a real-time understanding and adaptation that is rare in traditional coaching settings.

As leaders engage with horses and receive HRV feedback, they encounter a living barometer of their ability to regulate emotions and exert a calm influence. This interaction is not only about self-improvement, but also about learning how one's emotional state can influence and lead others without verbal communication. The non-verbal dialogue between humans and horses can be a powerful metaphor for the nuances of leadership, where presence, energy and authenticity often speak louder than words. Research by King and Hemsworth (2020) reinforces this perspective, highlighting the significant impact that human interaction has on horse behavior and welfare. When this knowledge is applied to leadership development, it becomes clear that the qualities that make for a successful leader—such as empathy, patience and clarity—are reflected in how one interacts with the horse. The horse's response provides immediate feedback on the effectiveness of these qualities, offering a practical and embodied experience of leadership in action.

By combining horses' sensitivity with biofeedback's precision, leaders are presented with a unique opportunity for growth. This transformative journey is about acquiring new skills and a fundamental shift in understanding leadership as an embodied, relational and responsive practice. The HRV biofeedback data bridges the cognitive and the visceral between understanding leadership concepts and feeling them in action. As leaders become more adept at interpreting and responding to HRV feedback in the presence of horses, they cultivate a heightened sense of emotional intelligence and regulation that is directly transferable to their human interactions. The equine-assisted biofeedback sessions thus become a microcosm of the leadership landscape, where the leader learns to balance directive presence with empathetic attunement, embracing the dual demands of modern leadership roles. Through this innovative approach, leaders are equipped to navigate the complexities of organizational life with a newfound sense of poise and authenticity, benefiting both themselves and those they lead.

The integration of biofeedback into coaching sessions with horses opens up a realm of possibilities for self-awareness and leadership growth. During these integrated sessions, several techniques can be incorporated to enhance self-regulation and emotional intelligence. These sessions provide a fertile ground for translating the science of HRV and controlled breathing into practical exercises that promote a leader's personal development.

Mindfulness and Grounding Exercises in a Global Cultural Context

Integrating biofeedback into leadership development is gaining momentum globally, reflecting its universality and efficacy across diverse cultures. While implementation varies across regions, biofeedback successfully addresses common leadership challenges related to stress, emotional regulation and mindfulness. This burgeoning worldwide perspective enriches the practice, contributing to a more inclusive, culturally attuned approach to developing self-aware, grounded leaders.

Fundamentally, biofeedback helps leaders become more aware of their internal states and stress responses. The real-time physiological data provides concrete insights that allow leaders to recognize unproductive reactions and purposefully self-regulate. Research shows that techniques incorporating biofeedback metrics such as HRV help leaders manage stress, focus attention and stay composed under pressure (Laborde, Mosley & Thayer, 2017). These benefits resonate across cultures, although the integration with local contexts differs. In Western cultures, biofeedback is often embraced as a scientifically validated technique, boosted by recent healthcare and wearable technology innovations. Meanwhile, in Eastern cultures with long traditions of meditation, yoga and energy practices, biofeedback is seen as complementing these ancient self-development tools. For instance, in China and India, biofeedback is combined with traditional practices, balancing modern science and ancient wisdom.

Illustrative case studies showcase this global perspective in action. In Japan, corporate leaders combining biofeedback and mindfulness report enhanced decision-making and lowered stress. In South Africa, biofeedback helped leaders become more emotionally intelligent and self-aware. In the United Arab Emirates, biofeedback training improved leaders' communication abilities and stress coping. Customizing biofeedback methods to resonate with cultural values is critical for success. For example, in communally oriented societies, sessions should emphasize group coherence and collective leadership. With indigenous communities, biofeedback should integrate holistic wellness perspectives. Training culturally fluent practitioners is key.

Localized integration enriches the practice and addresses leadership needs specific to cultural contexts. For instance, in parts of Asia and Latin America where hierarchy and saving face are valued, biofeedback helps leaders become more aware of stress responses to mitigate reactive, face-threatening behaviors. In Scandinavia's flatter, transparent culture, it builds skills for direct communication and authenticity.

Leaders worldwide can begin with foundational mindfulness practices to cultivate present-centered awareness and attunement to themselves and others, including horses in equine therapy. Grounding exercises where leaders stand quietly with a horse, feeling their connection with the earth, can induce relaxation while non-verbally bonding with the horse. Breathwork synchronized with the horse's rhythms likewise promotes interpersonal attunement.

Once ample mindfulness skills are cultivated, biofeedback can provide the next layer of insight. Here, wearable technology enters the field to reveal subconscious stress reactions. Reviewing biofeedback data allows leaders to identify triggers, understand their stress physiology and build self-regulation capacity. Targeted techniques such as HRV-guided breathing can facilitate relaxation responses amidst leadership challenges.

With advanced integration, machine learning algorithms can uncover subtle patterns in leaders' biofeedback data over time and predict personal, emotional triggers. This enables greater self-awareness and pre-emptive strategies to maintain equilibrium under pressure. For coaches, AI-assisted biofeedback analytics provide deeper insights to inform personalized interventions. While promising, care must be taken to implement biofeedback ethically across diverse contexts. Individual privacy and confidentiality of sensitive data should be safeguarded. There are also risks of mechanistic over-reliance on biofeedback metrics without nuanced human interpretation. Culturally informed coaching can mitigate these risks.

Integrative biofeedback strategies allow leaders worldwide to harness technology's advantages while remaining grounded in humanistic values tailored to local contexts. The future points to increased global connectivity and collaboration between diverse practitioners to share best practices. With skilled implementation and cultural awareness, biofeedback holds immense potential to develop more enlightened, purpose-driven leaders worldwide.

Guided Visualization Aligned with Personalized Leadership Goals

Guided visualization represents an integral element within biofeedback interventions for leadership growth. Leaders are encouraged to envision calming scenarios or mentally rehearse high-pressure situations while monitoring physiological metrics like HRV. This technique effectively bridges the gap between cultivated relaxation states and deploying equanimity amidst real-world leadership challenges. Biofeedback programming requires recognizing a leader's uniqueness and customizing it to targeted learning goals for optimal leadership development. A one-size-fits-all approach has limited viability in this context. Personalized biofeedback protocols are designed to pinpoint and address each leader's specific developmental needs and opportunities for growth. This customization enhances the coaching process, rendering it more meaningful and potent.

For example, an executive may undertake a tailored biofeedback curriculum with exercises concentrated on HRV training. This focus develops awareness around personal stress responses and strategies for effective management. The customized program enables the leader to track and analyze physiological reactions to stressors, driving profound and enduring positive changes in leadership behavior and capabilities. This targeted methodology has demonstrated significant improvements in stress resilience, emotional regulation and decision-making under pressure. Biofeedback can strategically concentrate on particular leadership growth areas, enhancing team leadership or building conflict management skills. This ensures the coaching moves beyond physiological self-mastery to target leadership behavioral changes and professional development outcomes.

Most standard biofeedback approaches emphasize self-regulation utilizing metrics like skin conductance and HRV. However, this intervention focused on engaging the leader in personalized exercises to recognize physiological cues in real leadership scenarios and interactions. This innovative approach enhanced relationship management and attunement to others' emotions. Adopting a holistic lens ensures biofeedback training complements leadership development activities such as workshops, mentoring and simulations. Integrating guided visualization into these personalized biofeedback initiatives allows leaders to intentionally practice and refine their emerging capabilities within a controlled, low-risk environment. This solidifies the likelihood these skills will successfully translate into authentic leadership contexts.

For instance, guided imagery may involve visualizing and giving an important presentation while monitoring stress reactions through HRV biofeedback sensors. Reviewing the physiological data afterward provides concrete insights into personal stress hot spots, for example during public speaking. The leader can then mentally rehearse the scenario while utilizing targeted breathing techniques. This builds vital stress-management skills, enabling the leader to stay composed in high-stakes speeches.

Personalized integration of biofeedback, guided visualization and existing leadership training modalities offers several advantages. It allows focus on a leader's unique growth needs rather than generic skills. It enhances metacognition and awareness of subconscious reactions that may sabotage leadership presence. Leaders also develop more robust self-regulation capacities. The results are flexible, agile leaders who embody resilience and emotional maturity to navigate complex challenges.

However, care must be taken to avoid overdependence on technology. Biofeedback should supplement, not replace, human-centered coaching. Practitioners must guard against becoming reductionist or prioritizing metrics over individual nuances. Ethical implementation requires understanding the limits of biofeedback and keeping the leader's whole being in view.

Strategically tailored biofeedback interventions, anchored in guided visualization, provide high-impact development for emerging leaders. Personalization enhances meaning, while guided imagery bridges the gap between cultivation and real-world application. This empowers leaders to transcend reactive tendencies and operate from a place of control and poised authenticity. With skilled guidance, biofeedback's possibilities for catalyzing growth are only beginning to be tapped. Leaders who harness these potentials with wisdom and humanity will be well-equipped to meet tomorrow's challenges with vision, innovation and purpose.

Rhythmic Movement Activities and the Challenges of Biofeedback in Coaching

Engaging leaders in attuned, rhythmic movement with horses—like grooming or walking in sync—provides a compelling developmental opportunity. Synchronizing to the horse's pace and energy requires profound presence and responsiveness, which can enhance HRV and emotional regulation—vital skills for effective leadership.

However, thoughtfully integrating biofeedback into equine coaching also surfaces complex limitations requiring diligent navigation. Biofeedback has introduced a pioneering methodology to coaching, especially in leadership development contexts. Still, implementation necessitates grappling with technical constraints and ethical dilemmas around client data privacy and interpretation. For instance, biofeedback accuracy varies based on equipment, potentially impacting data reliability. Inaccurate readings may prompt misguided interpretations and interventions, underscoring the need for high-caliber, clinically validated technology.

The learning curve can also be steep for clients, particularly those less technologically adept. Biofeedback efficacy relies heavily on clients actively engaging in learning and implementing techniques. Coaches must creatively demystify complex concepts and tailor delivery to match clients' learning preferences. This challenge is compounded due to tremendous individual variability in biofeedback responsiveness, attributed to psychological and physiological differences.

Ethical questions arise when collecting and leveraging clients' intimate physiological data. Coaches bear responsibility for safeguarding confidentiality and utilizing the data exclusively to enrich coaching. Robust data encryption, access limitations and informed consent protocols are essential. Over-reliance on biofeedback devices for self-regulation is another risk requiring mitigation. Coaches should emphasize lasting skills so clients can regulate emotions independently without excessive tech dependence. Avoiding reductionist tendencies that prioritize metrics over human complexity is crucial.

Competent interpretation and biofeedback data integration into coaching also relies on extensive skill development. Misinterpretations can prompt ineffective or even counterproductive strategies. Mastering biofeedback pre-requisites and artfully translating insights into coaching conversations demands rigorous training. In certain contexts, biofeedback integration may be inadvisable or impractical. In equine settings, wearing sensors may encumber interactions. Some clients may lack adequate self-awareness to benefit from biofeedback. Determining appropriate timing and tools remains the coach's responsibility.

Carefully selecting metrics and creating personalized protocols is also key. While HRV provides a window into stress physiology, additional biomarkers like skin temperature enrich the picture. Coaches must determine and justify the most useful data to address each client's needs while avoiding extraneous monitoring.

To leverage the advantages of biofeedback while mitigating limitations, coaches can:

- Invest in high-caliber, clinically validated equipment and stay updated on technological advances to enhance data relevance.
- Pursue extensive training in biofeedback basics, ethics and applications to ensure judicious integration.
- Educate clients using simple language and experiential learning. Ensure readiness to engage meaningfully.
- Co-design personalized protocols aligned tightly with leadership development goals. Avoid one-size-fits-all practices.
- Interpret data cautiously and holistically. Look at trends, not isolated data points.
- Secure informed consent and relentlessly protect data privacy through encryption, access limits and transparency.
- Monitor dependence and build lasting self-regulation skills that translate beyond sessions. Avoid mechanistic over-reliance.

While rhythmic equine activities offer impactful leadership development through HRV and emotional attunement, carefully navigating the complex-ities of biofeedback integration remains imperative. With skill, wisdom and ethics, coaches can unlock biofeedback's immense potential for catalyzing growth while honoring our shared humanity.

Biofeedback-Guided Breathing Exercises

Integrating biofeedback-guided breathing exercises into coaching sessions represents a pivotal component within leadership development programs. This approach involves coaching leaders in specific breathing techniques that can directly influence their real-time HRV, furnishing a powerful mechanism for self-regulation and emotional mastery. For instance, leaders may practice diaphragmatic breathing, concentrating inhales and exhales in the belly rather than shallower chest breathing. This methodology effectively stimulates the parasympathetic nervous system, eliciting a state of calm and relaxation. Leaders can use biofeedback devices to monitor their HRV as they breathe diaphragmatically, gaining instant feedback on how this style impacts their heart rate. This provides experiential insight into how breathing patterns affect physiology.

Leaders learn to modify their breathing rhythm and depth to optimize HRV, aiming for psychophysiological coherence—a state marked by harmony between the nervous, cardiovascular and respiratory systems. Research shows achieving coherence through paced breathing can enhance cognitive faculties, emotional balance and stress resilience. Some leaders may benefit from straightforward rhythmic breathing, steadily inhaling and exhaling at a controlled pace. Others may respond better to guided visualization paired with breathwork, envisioning serene images while managing their breathing. Personalized protocols tailored to needs and learning styles prove most effective.

Beyond sessions, biofeedback-guided breathing offers leaders a practical tool to recalibrate anytime. With regular practice, these techniques become easily accessible and portable, enhancing a leader's capacity to regain composure and clarity amidst daily stressors. Over time, dedicated breathing practice contributes to lasting gains in emotional regulation and well-being.

The real-time HRV feedback confirms how breathing impacts the stress response, reinforcing learning. As leaders observe their heart rate rhythms smooth out through proper breathing, this builds motivation to adopt the techniques. The visual interface of many wearable biofeedback devices further engages technology-fluent leaders. Effective integration relies on coaching leaders first in foundational pranayama breathing methods, from Yogic practice, without biofeedback. Once established, biofeedback sensors can be introduced to strengthen the technique and internalize learning through HRV monitoring. Progressing gradually avoids overdependence on technology.

Skilled practitioners artfully weave biofeedback into coherent narratives that empower sustained behavior change. For example, a coach could guide a stressed leader through a quick, coherent breathing exercise before an essential meeting while monitoring the leader's HRV. Afterward, the coach facilitates reflection on how regulating physiology aids focus and presence. Over time, such integration bridges episodic practices into lasting lifestyle shifts. The capacity to rapidly self-regulate the inner self empowers leaders to meet challenges with emotional agility and centered clarity. For instance, after a workplace conflict, a leader could find a quiet space, take a few minutes for coherent breathing assisted by HRV biofeedback, then return to the situation with renewed composure and solutions-focused attention.

Additionally, leaders can utilize mobile apps synced with wearable sensors to log breathing exercises and review historical HRV patterns. This metacognitive practice reveals personal stress triggers and successful regulation strategies. It also enables tracking progress over time, further motivating consistency. However, coaches must ensure technology enhances, not replaces, human connection and wisdom. While holding great potential, limitations warrant acknowledgment. Some leaders with trauma may feel triggered or flooded by prolonged attention to their physiology. The coach's skill and psychological safety are vital in such cases. Leaders also risk becoming dependent on biofeedback, underscoring the importance of internalizing skills for application anytime, anywhere.

Moving forward, leadership development integrating biofeedback-based breathing training with experiential, strengths-based coaching offers a high-impact pathway for growth. The possibilities span from building resilience during volatility to recovering optimally after setbacks. With astute personalization, compassionate guidance and ethical implementation, this methodology provides leaders with scientifically grounded yet profoundly humanizing tools for navigating complexity with wisdom, purpose and grace.

Emotionally Reflective Interaction Enhanced by Biofeedback and Emotional Intelligence

Leaders participating in equine-assisted development are encouraged to engage in emotionally reflective interactions with horses, recognizing and naming the emotions arising within them. Paired with HRV biofeedback, this fosters deeper awareness of how feelings manifest physically within the body. It also equips leaders to regulate emotional reactions more adaptively. The intricate linkage between biofeedback and emotional intelligence growth in leadership contexts is foundational. Biofeedback technologies specifically enhance core components of emotional intelligence, including self-regulation, social skills, empathy and self-awareness. For instance, self-awareness involves understanding one's emotions, values, strengths and weaknesses. Here, biofeedback acts as a mirror, illuminating the physiological footprints of emotions so leaders can better comprehend their inner terrain.

This expanded self-awareness represents the initial step for leaders to recognize emotional triggers and progress in intelligence. Self-regulation, vital for effective leadership, is where biofeedback tools prove invaluable. They furnish real-time feedback so leaders can witness how emotions impact their leadership across diverse situations. For example, noticing an HRV spike during a tense negotiation signals the leader to deploy breathing techniques or mindfulness to maintain rationality. Additionally, biofeedback aids leaders in building empathy, enhancing their awareness and presence during interactions to foster robust connections with team members. It also refines practical social skills, helping leaders become more cognizant of physiological cues embedded in non-verbal communication. This understanding guides leaders to refine their communication style for optimal resonance and rapport.

Training sessions can incorporate role-plays where leaders rehearse pressure scenarios while observing their biometric feedback. These experiences grant insights into blind spots and automatic reactions that are often hard to perceive otherwise. With *supportive* guidance, this builds self-efficacy to lead with authenticity.

By combining reflective equine interactions with biofeedback insights, leaders can cultivate profound emotional intelligence and move toward more attuned, ethical, compassionate leadership. The potential spans from regulated thinking under fire to recovering optimally from setbacks through composure. However, certain limitations warrant consideration. Some leaders may feel uncomfortable examining vulnerable emotions or sharing biometric data. Coaches must establish clear protocols and psychological safety for *voluntary* participation. Leaders also risk becoming dependent on biofeedback for self-awareness rather than cultivating a mindful presence. Guiding leaders to listen to innate body wisdom remains vital.

Importantly, overemphasis on physiology alone risks losing the human focus. Coaches must remind leaders that biofeedback serves only as an information stream, not the complete story. Bringing compassion and emotional attunement to interpret the data in context is critical. Integrating emotionally reflective equine experiences with biofeedback under professional guidance promises to unlock breakthrough leadership development. But foremost, the work must honor our shared humanity. With care, ethics and wisdom, biofeedback provides leaders an invaluable window into self-mastery, purpose and service.

Resilience Training

Resilience training is also integrated into these sessions, where leaders are exposed to mild stressors in the presence of the horse and guided to use biofeedback cues to return to a state of emotional and physiological balance. This could involve facing uncertainties or unpredictabilities in the horse's behavior and learning to maintain composure through focused breathing and mindfulness. Each of these techniques is enhanced by the immediate feedback provided by HRV monitoring, allowing for a tailored approach that meets each leader's unique needs and learning styles. The goal of each session is to teach techniques and embody them, creating muscle memory for emotional regulation that leaders can draw upon in their professional roles.

Incorporating these biofeedback techniques in equine-assisted activities not only enhances leaders' emotional intelligence and self-regulation skills, but also deepens their understanding of how to maintain balance and coherence in the face of leadership challenges. Through biofeedback-enhanced interaction with horses, leaders learn to translate physiological awareness into emotional and behavioral changes, leading to a more resilient and empathetic approach to leadership.

The session structure is designed to be iterative and reflective, allowing the client to gradually build upon their skills and deepen their understanding of the interplay between their physiological state, emotional regulation and leadership effectiveness. The presence of the horse is instrumental in this process, acting as both a catalyst for heightened self-awareness and a barometer for the efficacy of the biofeedback techniques employed. This unique combination of biofeedback and equine-assisted activities provides a powerful conduit for leadership transformation.

The Influence of Biofeedback and Adaptive Leadership Training Through Bio-NeuroFeedback

Biofeedback emerges as a pivotal tool in leadership development, profoundly impacting the neurological foundations of leadership behaviors and decision-making. Leaders are like conductors of a neural orchestra, with crucial brain regions such as the prefrontal cortex, responsible for complex cognitive behaviors, and the amygdala and hippocampus, which play central roles in emotional behavior and stress response, respectively. Biofeedback assists leaders in monitoring and controlling these emotional and stress responses, thereby indirectly influencing the activity within these critical brain regions.

Biofeedback takes a groundbreaking leap forward when integrated with neurofeedback, such as EEG technology, which measures brainwave activity. This integration provides real-time insights into brainwave patterns and HRV, enabling leaders to become more aware of their body's responses to stressful or emotionally complex situations. This awareness reflects directly on their brain activity, allowing for more informed and adaptive decision-making. Adaptive leadership training, a practical framework for helping leaders and organizations adapt to challenging environments, is significantly enhanced when combined with these insights from bio-neurofeedback. By receiving real-time feedback on cognitive functioning and decision-making processes, leaders gain a deeper understanding of navigating ambiguity and change. This approach fosters adaptability in decision-making and enriches a leader's ability to respond to dynamic environments and scenarios effectively.

The innovative combination of adaptive leadership principles and bio-neurofeedback marks a new frontier in leadership training. This blend of leadership art and science holds the promise of navigating the complexities of modern organizational landscapes. It transforms leadership practices by harnessing the biological substrates of leadership and helping leaders become more attuned through biofeedback, thus enhancing their innate capacities and leading to overall leadership prowess.

As this field continues to evolve, future studies could explore the long-term impacts of this training on team dynamics and organizational performance. Integrating neuroscience and biofeedback in improving leadership practices opens a window into understanding and enhancing the biological underpinnings of effective leadership. Integrating biofeedback and neuro-feedback provides leaders with a toolkit to monitor their stress responses, emotional regulation and real-time decision-making. By understanding how their physiology impacts leadership behaviors, leaders can adapt their responses to be more effective. This emerging field marks an inflection point in unlocking the potential of the human brain to navigate complexity and lead effectively.

However, questions remain regarding translating lab-based bio-neurofeed-back training into real-world leadership scenarios. Controlled settings with EEG and physiological monitoring equipment differ drastically from the unpredictable environments leaders face. Future research should explore how these training insights transfer to complex, rapidly evolving situations with competing priorities and uncertainty.

Additionally, the role of individual differences poses an area warranting further investigation. People exhibit distinct physiology and psychological variations that shape stress reactivity and decision-making tendencies. A one-size-fits-all approach to bio-neuro leadership training risks failing to account for these individual variances. Instead, training protocols could be persona-lized and adapted based on a leader's unique cognitive profile. The costs associated with extensive physiological monitoring equipment also raise financial barriers for organizations seeking to implement wide-scale biofeed-back leadership training. However, consumer-grade wearable devices con-tinue to become more afforadable, while advancing in their ability to provide meaningful stress and health insights. As the technology evolves and becomes accessible, the practicality of deploying these techniques across entire leadership teams could become more feasible.

Finally, the deeply personal nature of harnessing one's physiology merits considerate approaches that build trust and psychological safety. Requiring leaders to confront potential neurological vulnerabilities requires environ-ments where they feel secure and supported. The sensitive delivery of bio-feedback insights allows for positive growth and learning rather than undermining leaders' confidence to lead amid stress or uncertainty. Integrat-ing biofeedback, neuroscience and leadership training marks a promising evolution in unlocking human potential, but questions remain regarding real-world applicability, individual differences, accessibility and building psychological safety. As science matures, this deeply personal nature of bio-neurofeedback calls for patient, compassionate and ethical applications that harness the brain's malleability for positive leadership growth while avoiding manipulation or coercion.

Remote Coaching and Virtual Sessions with Biofeedback

We live in an era where remote working and virtual interactions are becom-ing the norm, and integrating biofeedback into virtual coaching sessions presents challenges and unique opportunities. Biofeedback can be adapted in remote coaching settings, giving clients a new possibility to explore using innovative remote biofeedback tools, online platforms and apps that facilitate biofeedback sessions hosted remotely. In a virtual setting, coaching necessitates a better strategy to let biofeedback be controlled traditionally. Coaches rely on tools that clients can use independently, with data that can be shared remotely. This also requires both parties to be proficient enough with the technology and comfortable in a digital communication environment to ensure success.

While this approach involves the technological aspect, it requires a shift in coaching strategies and methodologies that's perfectly suitable for a remote interaction format.

Remote biofeedback has various tools that can be used independently and from home. These can include wearable devices capable of monitoring HRV, brain wave activity and skin conductance, transmitting the data generated from clients to coaches in real-time. This technological advancement enables a consistent and accurate coaching process, even in a remote environment. In a virtual coaching context, many platforms and apps are specifically designed for this. They offer user-friendly interfaces, allowing clients to record and share physiological data with their coaches.

All of these platforms usually come with equipment that is specialized with analytical tools. They help interpret data and make it easier for coaches to provide the proper guidance for their clients during their virtual coaching sessions.

The most critical part of these virtual coaching sessions is ensuring effective communication between coaches and clients. The coaches must maintain clear and empathetic behavior even during virtual client sessions. In this case, coaches might be leaning towards adding interactive webinars, video demonstrations or digital content to ensure that the clients can fully understand how to accurately use the biofeedback devices and interpret their data. The most challenging part is establishing trust and maintaining engagement while building a remote coaching relationship. Coaches must support and connect clients while building this relationship over digital channels. Interactive digital tools, regular check-ins and personalized feedback can establish a solid coach–client relationship.

Coaches and clients must be aware of any aspects needed to take appropriate measures to secure the transmission and storage of biofeedback data generated during remote sessions. At best, coaches should suggest that clients maintain platforms with robust protocols that are capable of safely storing sensitive data generated by these tools during the coaching sessions. Even though the sessions are entirely virtual, that shouldn't limit the coach from creating a customized and personalized biofeedback coaching experience for their clients. Coaches can leverage data analytics to tailor their strategies to meet each client's development needs.

The effectiveness of this approach is undeniable and proves a more effective and efficient coaching outcome that directly aligns with the client's physiological patterns. But, again, in terms of challenges, we become aware that lack of physical presence can also make it harder for a coach to redirect focus in the moment with a client who is procrastinating on the use of their biofeedback devices.

Coaches must be prepared to provide technical support and ensure their clients are comfortable and capable of using the technology independently. Integrating digital mindfulness exercises, virtual reality environments to help with stress management, and online cognitive-behavioral therapy modules can be beneficial. These integrations lead toward a holistic coaching experience, addressing different aspects of the client's journey. Of course, this training may need additional direction and development from the coach's perspective to be effectively delivered in a virtual setting.

The coach should focus on mastering biofeedback technology and developing engagement strategies, digital data analysis and practical virtual communication skills. Even though coaches and clients are both aware of the challenges taken in these virtual coaching sessions, they are also mindful that the integration of biofeedback significantly impacts the leadership development applied correctly throughout the coach–client journey. Integrating biofeedback into the virtual world offers a flexible and personalized approach to coaching. Many leaders who operate in the digital world are the perfect fit for these virtual coaching sessions, as they help them to drastically improve in their leadership positions.

Team Dynamics and the Use of Biofeedback Techniques

Team dynamics play a pivotal role in determining leaders' effectiveness and success. Integrating biofeedback into team development contexts provides valuable insights into team members' physiological responses during interactions. This enhanced awareness between leaders and team members can engender clearer communication and more constructive dialogue. Specifically, biofeedback training can strengthen empathy by heightening awareness to emotional states. For example, HRV training helps cultivate calmness and attentive listening. When team members become more cognizant of others' emotional responses and triggers, they can better empathize. In this way, team members who can sense others' feelings can forge an inclusive climate where everyone feels safe and understood. At its essence, this methodology harbors profound potential to deepen understanding of people's emotional landscapes.

Applying biofeedback opens new pathways to enhanced communication, empathy and collaboration within team environments, becoming integral pillars of optimal team dynamics. Through biofeedback training, members can learn to regulate emotional reactions in ways that engender greater openness, trust and coordinated effort. For example, leaders can monitor their physiology using HRV biofeedback during team meetings and adjust their state to remain open and attentive. This creates space for perspectives to emerge while role-modeling emotional intelligence. Meanwhile, members can observe their stress responses and practice maintaining composure during tense exchanges.

The experience of learning and applying biofeedback techniques together also represents a team-building activity, fostering mutual understanding. When shared openly, these practices provide a communal touchpoint and reinforce a sense of cohesion. For benefits to endure, ongoing practice and integration are essential. One impactful approach is facilitating regular team coherence sessions where members reflect together on biofeedback data from a shared activity. These sessions offer opportunities to deepen relationships, normalize vulnerable discussions about stress and set collective intentions.

With time, practices utilized during formal workshops translate into everyday interactions. For instance, members may exchange subtle cues to take a few coherent breaths before responding to frustration. This builds the team's capacity to regulate collectively. Celebrating wins where emotional regulation and empathy-enhanced outcomes reinforce learning.

There are also limitations requiring consideration. Some members may not yet have the self-awareness for biofeedback training to resonate. The leader must foster psychological safety for voluntary participation. It is also vital to avoid mandating the disclosure of private physiological data to prevent coercion. Members may over-focus on data points rather than the human context, a tendency requiring redirection. Additionally, some teams may need foundational communication and trust-building before introducing biofeedback tools. Discerning appropriate timing is key.

Long-Term Impact and Future Trends of Biofeedback in Leadership Development

Biofeedback has solidified itself as a fundamental component within leadership development, chiefly aimed at furnishing leaders with techniques to understand and regulate their stress and emotional responses. Over time, and with dedicated practice, these tools can catalyze profound changes, including enhanced decision-making under pressure and improved interpersonal attunement. Leaders undertaking biofeedback training gain personal understanding while cultivating enduring shifts in perceiving and moderating their inner states.

To sustain benefits, consistent application during sessions and daily life is essential. For instance, in one case a leader demonstrated how she applied biofeedback techniques to navigate a turbulent merger successfully, showcasing her integration of learning. In another, a leader exhibited sustained improvements in leadership style and well-being over several years through ongoing biofeedback practice. Regular sessions and self-monitoring through biofeedback apps and devices are key to maintaining gains. Moreover, organizational cultures that encourage biofeedback use and peer support groups reinforce lasting adoption.

The future trajectory of biofeedback technology holds exciting potential to revolutionize leadership development applications. Biofeedback devices are expected to become more sophisticated and ubiquitous, with sensor-embedded smart fabrics allowing continuous, discreet monitoring. This would enable seamless integration of biofeedback insights into daily leadership routines. Combining biofeedback systems with artificial intelligence could enable predictive capabilities exceeding conscious awareness. Such technology could provide a pre-emptive analysis of impending stress or emotional reactions, allowing leaders to mitigate these responses proactively. As these innovations evolve, they will equip leaders with increasingly powerful self-regulation tools, enabling more agile, mindful responses to workplace demands.

However, while promising, care must be taken to avoid overdependence on technology. Biofeedback should augment, not substitute, human wisdom, empathy and discretion. Coaches have an ethical responsibility to help leaders develop self-mastery that transfers beyond devices. Bringing compassion and emotional attunement to the interpretation of data is also critical to avoid mechanistic applications.

There are also risks of confidentiality breaches with an extensive collection of intimate physiological data. Organizations implementing biofeedback systems must rigorously protect leaders' privacy and transparently communicate proper usage. Without diligent safeguards and guidance, leaders may distrust the technology's purpose, undermining engagement. Integrating biofeedback training into broader development programs focused on strengths, purpose and mindfulness may prove most fruitful for sustained adoption. When contextualized as one tool within a multifaceted curriculum, leaders recognize its contributions while avoiding obsessive reliance. Ongoing coaching helps leaders translate insights into authentic practice. Regular community of practice meetings where leaders share integration experiences and challenges can further enhance sustained, thoughtful usage.

Biofeedback unquestionably provides valuable information about self-awareness and self-mastery as a leadership competency. However, crafting supportive organizational cultures and development systems surrounding biofeedback training may matter just as much for long-term behavior change. With wisdom, ethics and compassion guiding implementation, biofeedback technology holds immense potential to develop more enlightened, purpose-driven leaders ready to shape a thriving future consciously.

Notes

1 Schwartz, M. S., & Andrasik, F. (2003). *Biofeedback: A practitioner's guide* (3rd ed.). Guilford Press.
2 Green, E., & Green A. (1989). *Beyond biofeedback.* Knoll Publishing Company.
3 Kim, H.-G., Cheon, E.-J., Bai, D.-S., Lee, Y. H., & Koo, B.-H. (2018). Stress and heart rate variability: A meta-analysis and review of the literature. *Psychiatric Investigation*, 15(3), 235–245.

4 Jacobson, E. (1929). *Progressive relaxation*. University of Chicago Press.
5 Smith, L. B., Cipriani, D., & Shklovskiy, G. M. (2019). Quantifying heart rate variability using smartphone-based photoplethysmography. *Journal of Medical Engineering & Technology*, 43(4), 269–279.
6 Laborde S., Mosley, E., & Thayer J. (2017). Heart rate variability and cardiac vagal tone in psychophysiological research: Recommendations for experiment planning, data analysis, and data reporting. *Frontiers in Psychology*, 8, 213.
7 More available at www.heartmath.org/research/.
8 More available at www.hrv4training.com/publications.html.
9 Gehrke, E. K., Baldwin, A., & Schiltz, P. (2011). Heart rate variability in horses engaged in equine-assisted activities. *Journal of Equine Veterinary Science*, 31(2), 78–84.

Chapter 3

Psychometric Profiling in Leadership Coaching

Introduction to Psychometric Profiling

Psychometric profiling is the systematic recording and analysis of a person's psychological and behavioral characteristics to thoroughly assess or predict the person's personality traits and abilities, as well as how these occur in a certain context or clear relation to other people. In this exploration, we extend the boundaries of psychometric profiling to encompass the realm of biofeedback and coaching with horses. This integration not only highlights the versatility of psychometric tools but also opens up new avenues for understanding leadership dynamics through the lens of biofeedback and equine-assisted learning. By merging together profiling, biometrics and the intuitive feedback from horses, this approach offers a novel perspective on enhancing human potential and leadership qualities.

Comprehensive profiling can be rigorously performed using various robust data sources, and specialized profiling tools make the methodical analysis process much more efficient, especially when dealing with large volumes of pertinent data, such as psychometric assessment tools.[1] Most profiling tools can accurately infer insightful relationships between multifaceted data points. They can be effectively utilized to thoroughly assess a person's qualities, preferred communication style, approach to conflict, contributions in a collaborative team environment, leadership style and cognitive ability. These informative psychometric resources can significantly assist individuals in making well-informed, evidence-based decisions about their current talent and the talent they need to develop. Additionally, these scientific resources can tremendously benefit organizations by allowing them to determine what skills to develop in their leaders systematically and which new employees to recruit based on strategic predictive profiling. Psychometric assessments enable organizations to optimize personnel selection and development to enhance productivity.

Psychometric profiling can provide a deeper understanding of and insights into:

- What motivates and excites people in the work they do
- How people are most likely to behave in various situations

DOI: 10.4324/9781032683843-4

- How to adapt behaviors according to the situation and business need
- How to allocate the right work to the right people, maximizing motivation and performance
- How people prefer to communicate and deal with conflict
- How people are likely to adapt or react to change
- What style of work is best for them in their career development or business
- People's strengths through increased awareness
- Behavioral strengths and weaknesses in interviews
- What additional team-building activities would be beneficial

With that in mind, psychometric profiling, a cornerstone in leadership coaching, is a scientific approach that quantifies an individual's capabilities and behavioral styles. It harnesses a range of assessments to map out personality traits, cognitive abilities and behavioral tendencies, offering a systematic way to gauge a leader's strengths and needed areas of development. This technique, rooted in the early work of psychologists like Charles Spearman and his concept of "g," or general intelligence, has matured into a sophisticated array of tools, including the Five Factor Model and the NEO Personality Inventory, which provide insights into how personality traits manifest in a leadership context.[2] Cognitive abilities are another focus of psychometric profiling, with tools like the WAIS and Raven's Progressive Matrices, which measure problem-solving and information processing, essential elements in understanding a leader's adaptability and strategic thinking capabilities. Behavioral tendencies, evaluated through instruments like the Thomas-Kilmann Instrument (TKI) or Myers Briggs Type Indicator (MBTI), further enrich the profile, revealing communication styles and decision-making preferences that inform leadership dynamics.[3]

These assessments are integral to a holistic coaching strategy, enabling leaders to understand how their attributes affect their leadership style and team interactions. This insight is crucial for tailoring development plans that leverage a leader's strengths and address their challenges, requiring coaches adept in psychometrics to provide the nuanced interpretation and support needed. The concept of crime profiling from criminology, which constructs psychological and behavioral profiles of criminals based on crime data and crime-scene analysis, when merged with psychometric profiling, ushers in a new dimension of predictive behavioral analysis in corporate settings. This combination paves the way for a forensic approach to identifying behaviors and traits linked with successful leadership, analogous to how crime profilers discern patterns and motives to predict future offenses.

Leadership assessment benefits from this integrated approach, where a meticulous analysis of a leader's career path and decision-making patterns can reveal the predictors of leadership success. Additionally, talent development can leverage this method by employing business case studies that mimic the intricacy of criminal cases, challenging aspiring leaders to navigate complex scenarios while their responses are scrutinized for not only content, but also for underlying thought processes, ethical considerations and risk management.

Applications of this blended methodology can manifest in various forms:

- **Behavioral Analysis for Team Dynamics:** Similar to the study of criminal networks, leadership profilers can dissect team dynamics to pinpoint emergent leaders, influencers and cohesiveness enhancers, which is vital for effective team assembly and leadership placement.
- **Crisis Simulation Exercises:** Taking a page from crime-scene simulations, leaders can be immersed in intricate crisis scenarios to assess their decision-making under duress, stress management and ethical judgment, reflecting the real-world challenges leaders face.
- **Forensic Organizational Reviews:** Echoing the crime profiler's task of scene reconstruction, post-event organizational reviews can dissect leaders' decisions and actions to unveil their strategic and managerial acumen during critical corporate milestones.

Marrying the analytical rigor of crime profiling with the psychological insights of psychometric assessments enables leadership coaches and organizational psychologists to forge a more multidimensional understanding of leadership capacity and performance predictors. This integration of forensic and psychometric profiling transcends conventional assessments, offering a richer, more intricate view of leadership potential by meticulously delving into the subtleties and nuances of human behavior and decision-making, and examining how these dynamics translate in a business context. It crafts an insightful leadership landscape where executives and managers are thoroughly assessed and deeply understood within settings that reflect the intricacy and uncertainty of their roles.

In leadership coaching and development, these integrated psychometric-forensic assessments are not used in isolation but as part of a comprehensive, evidenced-based coaching strategy designed to cultivate greater self-awareness, catalyze personal development and substantially enhance leadership effectiveness. By understanding their integrated psychometric-behavioral profile, leaders can gain valuable insight into how their innate personal attributes and tendencies may shape their leadership approach, team interactions, decision-making processes, and how they might be perceived by peers, team members and organizational stakeholders. However, the application of such in-depth psychometric profiling must be undertaken with expertise, rigor and sensitivity by leadership coaches, as it involves interpreting and benchmarking complex human cognitive, emotional and social characteristics within a career context. Coaches extensively trained in psychometrics and forensic profiling can provide leaders with the necessary context, interpretation guidance and ongoing support to comprehend their integrated profiles fully. This enables leaders to translate this multidimensional self-insight into tailored, measurable leadership development plans that precisely target enhancement opportunities, ensure continued growth in critical areas like emotional intelligence and provide an evidence-based trajectory for meeting leadership potential. When aggregated across groups of leaders, comprehensive psychometric-forensic profiles allow organizations to conduct predictive analytics using real-world career pattern data, assess current leadership bench strength and gaps, design ranking systems for high-potential leaders based on scientifically validated attributes of top performers, and construct targeted programs to bolster leadership pipelines. This application ushers in an analytics-enabled future for leadership coaching.

Understanding Personality and Behavioral Assessments

At the very core of psychometric profiling lies a meticulous and multidimensional exploration of human personality, motivation, emotional intelligence and behavior, when seen through the lens of organizational psychology. This fascinating field judiciously navigates through seminal debates within psychology literature, such as the degree of influence from heredity vs. environmental conditioning, the role of innate psychological dispositions vs. situational and socialization factors, and the impacts of gender, ethnicity, age and socio-historical perspectives on personality development and behavioral expression in a workplace context. To effectively and responsibly leverage the robust predictive power of modern psychometric assessments in talent screening, leadership development, succession planning and other organizational decisions, one must thoroughly comprehend the foundational psychological theories and empirical research that underpin these tools. This includes a nuanced understanding of the origins of personality frameworks, assessment validation processes and metrics for responsible usage.

A cardinal truth revealed by interdisciplinary research is that no two people are identical in their thoughts, motivations, decision-making patterns and leadership behaviors. Even genetically identical twins raised in the same household will display measurable differences in their cognitive processing styles, emotional regulation capabilities, interpersonal dynamics and overall leadership presence. Some individuals may have an inherent tendency towards anxiety and self-doubt, while others radiate calm and self-assurance. Some leaders may be gregarious and outgoing, readily connecting across organizational silos, while others are more introspective and content developing deep expertise in a specialized domain.

Personality, then, constitutes a person's unique "essence"—those entrenched, predictable patterns of tendencies by which we can recognize one leader from another and that largely persist over time and situations. Numerous definitions of personality exist within the psychology canon, but a commonly utilized concept is that personality represents the characteristic profile of thoughts, emotional orientation, motivations and behaviors that notably distinguish one person from another and demonstrate stability across various life stages.

Critically, personality encompasses more than merely observable actions—it also includes more subtle internal ruminations, beliefs, needs and preferences that profoundly shape the leadership approach. Additionally, personality is understood to exhibit high constancy over decades and circumstances, although individuals may sometimes behave unusually "out-of-character" due to intense situational pressures that test their adaptability. Leadership derailment events often reveal the more hidden aspects of personality in leaders lacking developmental self-awareness. While we all subconsciously develop informal theories of personality to simplify perceptions of colleagues through routine workplace interactions, the psychometric approach leverages scientifically validated personality frameworks, leadership competency models and career pattern analysis tools to deeply diagnose leadership capacity with sophistication and strong predictive power that surpasses informal assumptions. This contrasts causal inferences with a rigorous methodology grounded in statistical evidence, guaranteeing precise, reliable and ethical usage.

Additionally, influential concepts such as motivation, values, attitudes and beliefs may profoundly evolve over a leader's lifespan. In contrast, personality demonstrates substantially higher long-term stability, particularly when assessed with robust psychometric instruments designed to surface enduring traits.[4] Hence, psychometric profiling parses out multiple layers of psychological complexity, from mutable states to entrenched traits, to responsibly inform monumental talent decisions.

A multiparadigm academic grounding allows organizations to implement psychometric profiling with a consciousness of personality psychology origins, respect for the predictive limits of assessments, and an ethical, people-centered testing philosophy focused on potential realization over simplistic labeling. This is the foundation for responsible usage as psychometric profiling continues advancing as a decision science.

Thus:

Ability: An ability is the power to perform either a mental or physical act. At work, we tend to be concerned with cognitive or physical abilities, such as verbal reasoning, numerical reasoning, spatial ability, manual dexterity, etc.

Motivation: These phenomena are involved in the operation of incentives, drives and motives. Motivation is the internal force that activates our behavior and directs it toward one goal or another. In this way, for example, one's over-riding motivation might be material rewards, and the direct result of this might be a salary increase (the motive). Depending on a person's theoretical stance, these drives may be more or less mutable.

Values: Values are a function of a person's moral principles or beliefs and represent the desirability, worth, and importance that the individual places upon them.

Attitudes: Attitudes are a more or less stable set of opinions, interests or purposes that involve the expectancy of a certain experience. Typically, an attitude represents how we behave toward someone or something with an underlying evaluation tone.

Beliefs: A belief is a special attitude or feeling that acknowledges or recognizes a statement is true or something as real.

A vast range of internal and external factors combine to create individual personalities. The challenge facing us as students of human personality is to try to unravel the contribution of genetic and environmental influences. For example, a trait such as aggression is a prime case in point. Many studies have pointed to aggression as an inherited characteristic, whereas other studies have also found relationships between peer pressure, temperature, body size and child-rearing practices. It would seem that genetic factors may also influence how we interact with our environment.

Increasingly, however, there is strong evidence for genetic factors being a major contributor to particular personality characteristics. One of the favored research techniques is the study of twins. Identical, or monozygotic, twins are siblings whose genetic makeup is identical, so, for example, if one twin has dark hair, the other has dark hair. Some consistent findings in identical-twin studies show a significant degree of inheritability for traits such as neuroticism and extraversion. For neuroticism, the genetic impact is even more marked in females. Twin studies also demonstrate that schizophrenia has a strong genetic component. Genetic/biological impacts include:

- Extraversion
- Neuroticism
- Aggression
- Criminality
- Schizophrenia
- Positivity or negativity
- Sociability
- Activity
- Emotionality

Hans Eysenck's seminal research on fundamental extraversion/introversion dispositions suggests that introverts have an inherently higher basal rate of cortical arousal in the brain than extroverts.[5] Consequently, the introvert personality type feels a constant underlying drive to reduce external stimulus exposure from the environment to maintain an optimal level of arousal. In contrast, extroverts perpetually seek out further external stimulation due to their lower basal arousal.

Rigorous biological studies on the neuroendocrinology underlying personality have found that heightened aggression has an empirically verified linkage with substantially elevated levels of testosterone in both males and females. For example, multiple studies have shown that pregnant women carrying male babies (and thus, exposed to higher in-utero testosterone secretion) report significantly higher levels of aggressive ideations and irritation than their pregnant peers carrying female babies. Additionally, the neurotransmitter dopamine plays a key role in generalized reward-seeking behaviors and experiencing positive emotions, while serotonin critically influences the regulation of negativity in emotional responses.

Recent research on unrelated, adopted children and twins reveals that enduring antisocial tendencies and criminal behavior have a significant genetic component. By comparing twins' behavior and studying adopted children, scientists challenge the previous belief that these traits were solely influenced by the environment. This groundbreaking work highlights the complex interplay between genetics and environment in shaping human behavior. Additionally, longitudinal studies tracking the lifespans of intellectually gifted children have revealed that certain facets of cognitive ability, such as verbal acuity, also have a genetic origin. Concurrently, behavioral genetic studies of newborn babies have persuasively concluded that three fundamental temperamental dispositions are innately present at birth—(a) stimulus reactivity and emotional intensity, (b) motor activity levels, and (c) appetitive social motivation and sociability—which act as predictive harbingers of later academic attitudes, achievement, and classroom behaviors.[6] For example, infants who are constitutionally less physically active, less socially motivated, and more emotionally reactive and distressed tend to have a more withdrawn temperament, demonstrate higher sensitivity, and are often slower to warm up to novel learning stimuli and social situations positively. However, personalized early interventions tailored to temperament can substantially improve outcomes.

In total, the maturation of personality and behavioral genetics as scientific disciplines has extensively discredited prior "blank slate" philosophies that downplayed innate dispositions. We now possess overwhelming evidence that personality and behavior have important biological underpinnings that interact with experience to shape outcomes. Organizational psychology assessments account for both components.

Age, Gender and Ethnicity

Recent research has significantly deepened our understanding of human personality traits, exploring whether men and women exhibit consistent differences, how personality varies across ethnicities, and the stability and changeability of these traits over time.[7]

Meta-analyses reveal that while there are gender differences in certain traits,[8] overall, men and women have similar personality profiles. For instance, women generally score higher in traits like anxiety and warmth, while men often show greater emotional stability and assertiveness. These differences diminish when adjusting for biases like social desirability, suggesting that socialization influences these traits more than biology alone. Additionally, cross-cultural research has shown that the structure of personality traits is consistent worldwide, emphasizing biological rather than ethnic influences, although cultural factors can influence behavioral expressions of these traits. Longitudinal studies indicate that personality stabilizes around age 30 but remains adaptable to significant life changes.

In the field of age-related personality changes, studies, including a prominent one from the University of California, Berkeley, suggest that traits like conscientiousness and agreeableness evolve throughout life, challenging the notion that personality is fixed after childhood. Notably, conscientiousness increases during one's 20s, and agreeableness changes most significantly in the 30s and continues into the 60s.

Research on gender differences using the Five Factor Model shows men typically score higher on traits like assertiveness and women higher on agreeableness and anxiety, with these differences reflecting both biological and social influences.

Ethnic research is less extensive but indicates that while some differences exist, cultural impacts are significant. This area remains cautiously studied due to concerns about potential misuse of findings.

Historical Views

While this chapter focuses on the psychometric approach to personality, no consideration of personality would be complete without looking at historical views and alternative theories, such as psychoanalysis, analytical psychology, humanistic psychology and social learning theory.

Physiology

Hippocrates (470–377 BCE) was born in Crete and is regarded as the father of medicine. Apart from his medical interests, he devised a physiological typology of personality that remained current in Europe until the 17th century. Hippocrates formed a view that personality was dictated by the preponderance of one of four special fluids in the body (the humors), namely:

- Black bile—depression, sleeplessness
- Yellow bile—angry, agitated

- Blood—sanguine, courageous
- Phlegm—calm, unemotional

In the 20th century, American psychologist William Sheldon developed a rather different physiological typology. Sheldon categorized individuals into three body types—endomorphic, mesomorphic and ectomorphic—based on extensive photographic and measurement analysis of nude figures. He also attributed specific personality traits to each of these body types:

- Endomorphic—overweight, soft, and round body types; relaxed, sociable
- Mesomorphic—muscular, rectangular, strong; energetic, assertive
- Ectomorphic—thin, long, fragile; artistic, introverted

Psychoanalysis

Any discussion of personality theory must acknowledge Sigmund Freud's significant contributions to our understanding of human psychology. Freud emphasized that all human actions, thoughts and feelings are meaningful and driven by underlying purposes. He outlined three levels of consciousness:

1 **Conscious:** This small yet immediate aspect of the mind encompasses what we are actively aware of, including thoughts and emotions that can be logically articulated and analyzed.
2 **Preconscious:** Acting as a bridge between conscious awareness and the unconscious, this layer contains ordinary memories that are not actively in thought but can be easily accessed.
3 **Unconscious:** The largest and most influential part of the mind, housing deep-seated impulses and desires governed by the id, ego and superego.[9]

Freud's model of the mind comprises three interacting systems:

- **The Id:** Existing entirely within the unconscious, the id is driven by the pleasure principle, seeking immediate gratification for basic needs and desires.
- **The Ego:** The ego develops from the id and operates under the reality principle. It assesses the real-world context and acts as a mediator between the desires of the id and the moral standards of the superego, aiming to find realistic ways to satisfy desires without negative consequences.
- **The Superego:** Emerging last, the superego encompasses the moral standards learned from parents and society. It strives for perfection by enforcing ethical conduct and generating feelings of guilt or anxiety when we fail to meet its standards.

Freud also described psychosexual stages of development, each focusing on different erogenous zones and themes:

- **Oral Stage (birth–18 months):** Focus on mouth activities like sucking, with themes of dependency. Issues here can lead to adult traits of passivity or dependence.
- **Anal Stage (18 months–3.5 years):** Centered on bowel control, with themes of obedience and self-control. Fixation might result in adults who are either overly organized or defiantly disorganized.
- **Phallic Stage (3.5–6 years):** Involves genital awareness and the Oedipus/ Electra complexes, with themes of sexual identification and morality. Fixations here can affect adult sexual attitudes and behaviors.
- **Latency Stage (6 years to puberty):** A phase of diminished sexual impulses where energy is focused on social and intellectual skills.
- **Genital Stage (post-puberty):** Focuses on mature sexual relationships and the balance between love and work.

Despite the groundbreaking nature of Freud's theories, they have been critiqued for lack of empirical support, overemphasis on sexual motivations, pessimistic views of human nature, and the deterministic approach that may undervalue environmental and contextual factors. Freud's ideas, though foundational, are often seen as outdated in the light of modern psychological research which calls for a more nuanced understanding of personality development.

Humanistic Psychology

Humanistic psychology shifts away from the idea that people are driven by instincts or archetypes, as suggested by psychoanalytic theories, and instead emphasizes individual perceptions and understandings of events. This approach suggests that people, much like scientists, actively interpret their world and test their interpretations through experiences. George Kelly, a pivotal figure in this field, proposed that everyone acts as a "scientist" in daily life by forming, testing and refining hypotheses about their reality.

Kelly's theory is organized around a central postulate and 11 corollaries. His fundamental postulate states that a person's psychological processes are shaped by their expectations of future events. This mirrors the scientific method of moving from hypothesis to experimentation. Kelly's corollaries further elaborate how personal constructs, or individual interpretations of experiences, govern behavior. These constructs are dichotomous, meaning they often have two contrasting options, like "good-bad," and are organized systematically to aid in predicting outcomes.

The corollaries also describe how these constructs adapt over time based on new experiences, thus continually reshaping our anticipations and behaviors. For instance, the Modulation Corollary highlights that some constructs are more open to change than others. Additionally, the Choice Corollary explains that individuals select behaviors based on what they believe will most likely enhance their understanding and ability to anticipate future events.

Kelly emphasizes that each person's construct system is unique, but similarities can exist, particularly within cultural contexts. His theory acknowledges the complexity of human psychology by noting that individuals can hold multiple, sometimes conflicting, constructs and still function in society by understanding and relating to others' viewpoints.

Thus, humanistic psychology, through Kelly's personal construct theory, views individuals as active interpreters of their worlds, emphasizing the role of personal agency and psychological flexibility. This approach is inherently personal and subjective, focusing on the individual's perspective, and is shaped significantly by the therapist's skill in understanding and applying the theoretical framework.

Social Learning Theory

The origins of social learning are generally ascribed to Julian Rotter. An experienced clinical psychologist, like many in the early 1950s, Rotter was concerned with developing a theory that would help us understand and predict behavior in a *social* setting. Rotter's Social Learning Theory posits that a wide array of potential behaviors is available to us in any given situation, each with its likelihood of occurrence based on appropriateness and potential outcomes. This theory encompasses all forms of behavior, including motor acts, thoughts, verbal and non-verbal expressions, and emotional responses.

> **Expectancy and Behavior:** A key tenet of Rotter's theory is that behavior is not just a reaction to conditioning but involves anticipatory and cognitive processes. Humans actively think about and predict the consequences of their actions, choosing behaviors they believe will yield the most desirable outcomes. This decision-making process is influenced by our expectations of the likelihood of achieving specific reinforcements.
>
> **Reinforcement Value:** Rotter introduces the concept of reinforcement value to explain the subjective appeal of different outcomes. We are more likely to engage in behaviors that lead to outcomes we find desirable or rewarding. Conversely, outcomes that are unappealing have a low reinforcement value and are less likely to be pursued, even if the likelihood of achieving them is high.
>
> **Psychological Situation:** Rotter emphasizes the importance of the context in which behaviors occur. He argues that the effectiveness of a behavior and the value of its potential reinforcements can vary significantly across

different situations. This situational perspective helps explain why certain behaviors are more effective or desired in one context than another.

Despite its contributions to understanding the interaction between individual actions and social contexts, Rotter's theory has faced criticism for not forming a comprehensive theory of personality. Critics argue that it focuses more on explaining specific behaviors rather than overarching personality traits. Additionally, the theory has been noted for its lack of emphasis on biological and genetic factors and for not providing objective measures of personality from a social learning standpoint.

With that in mind, Rotter's Social Learning Theory integrates cognitive and environmental factors to explain how behaviors are chosen and reinforced, highlighting the significant role of both individual expectations and situational contexts.

Behaviorism

Behaviorism, established by John B. Watson in the early 20th century with his pivotal 1913 publication "Psychology as the behaviorist views it," posits that all behavior is acquired through environmental interactions and conditioning, sidelining internal mental states in favor of observable actions. This school of psychology focuses on behaviors that can be observed and measured, employing controlled experiments and systematic observations that exclude subjective mental states such as thoughts and emotions.

The approach distinguishes two main types of conditioning: **Classical Conditioning**, where a natural stimulus is paired with a response, followed by the association of a neutral stimulus with the natural one until the neutral stimulus alone can evoke the response; and **Operant Conditioning**, which uses rewards and punishments to link behaviors with their consequences, thereby influencing behaviors based on the outcomes they produce.

Despite its origins, modern behaviorism has evolved to acknowledge the influence of internal states, yet it continues to focus on observable behaviors and measurable outcomes, retaining Watson's emphasis on empirical data. The strengths of behaviorism lie in its ability to provide quantifiable and observable data, making it easier to collect information and conduct research. It has also inspired effective behavioral interventions and therapies that are particularly effective in modifying undesirable behaviors.

However, behaviorism has been criticized for its simplistic approach that ignores internal motivations and mental states. It fails to account for types of learning that occur without direct reinforcement and does not adequately address the adaptability of behavior in response to new information. Despite these criticisms, behaviorism remains a fundamental, albeit contested, approach in psychology that prioritizes external actions and their measurable impacts over internal psychological experiences.

Psychometric Theory

Thus far, this chapter has highlighted the extent to which many researchers approached the subject of personality theory from a clinical point of view. Equally of interest, the development of many theories has had less to do with scientific methodology and more with an intuitive or "armchair" approach.

In the realm of psychometrics, clients are viewed as "normal," and the focus is on understanding how personality variables influence behavior and preferences in the workplace. The psychometric approach to personality emphasizes the scientific measurement of human characteristics, adhering to rigorous methodologies that include quantification of variables, use of representative samples, precise statistical analysis and clear research designs. The theories advanced in psychometric research are constructed to be testable and refutable.

Psychometric assessments of personality are broadly categorized into type theory and trait theory. Type theory, exemplified by Carl Jung's work, groups individuals based on shared behavioral characteristics. This approach, while inclusive and useful in counseling settings, is often critiqued for its limited exploration of personality dimensions and potential for labeling, which may not be useful in diverse workplace settings.

Trait theory, on the other hand, posits that all individuals possess the same traits to varying degrees. This theory is considered non-inclusive and views traits as stable behavioral tendencies observable across different situations. Trait-based assessments are prevalent in workplace environments for selection, development and career guidance because they allow for the identification of distinct individual differences.

Critics of trait theory point out challenges related to the theoretical and design robustness of questionnaires, the complexity of integrating multiple behavioral dimensions, and the variability of out-of-character behaviors. Despite these challenges, trait theory has been foundational in psychometrics, with pioneers like Gordon Allport and Raymond Cattell making significant contributions. Allport introduced a hierarchy of traits ranging from cardinal traits, which dominate an individual's personality, to central and secondary traits, which describe more specific qualities and situational behaviors. Cattell's factor analytic approach further refined the understanding of traits, distinguishing between source traits that fundamentally drive behaviors and more superficial traits that vary with circumstances.

Overall, the psychometric view in psychology uses structured, scientific methods to measure and understand personality, providing valuable tools for assessing individual differences in various contexts, especially within the workplace.

The Big Five

Recently, numerous scholars have employed factor analysis to support a theoretical framework consisting of five primary traits inherent to varying extents in all individuals. These traits are typically considered consistent over time. For instance, neuroticism is one of these enduring traits, which contrasts with fleeting personality states like the anxiety one might feel before a driving test. Further on, we will explore the concept of the Big Five more thoroughly.

Traits vs. Competencies

Understanding the difference between personality traits and competencies is crucial. Traits refer to consistent patterns of behavior, thought and emotion. For instance, introversion is a trait marked by shyness, reserve and withdrawal. Competencies, on the other hand, are behaviors and technical skills essential for effective performance in a job setting. In management, competencies may involve building relationships, networking, and leveraging contacts. While the trait of extraversion may contribute to these competencies, it is not the only determinant of successful performance.

Understanding How to Measure Personality

The effectiveness of psychometric profiling hinges on the careful selection and administration of assessments. Coaches are introduced to critical factors, including validity, reliability, cultural appropriateness, and the potential for bias, sabotage, or distortion. Administering assessments is an art in and of itself. Coaches must understand how to conduct these assessments, ensuring the process is ethical, respectful and informative.

The strengths and limitations of a range of methods are worth considering.

Projective Techniques

Projective techniques, such as the Rorschach Inkblot Test, originate from clinical settings and are designed to elicit spontaneous responses that reveal deep-seated perceptions. While they provide comprehensive insights into an individual's psyche, these methods suffer from issues like poor inter-rater reliability, lack of standardized norms, and are time-intensive in both administration and analysis.

Self-Report Questionnaires

Self-report questionnaires are widely used in the workplace due to their efficiency and ease of administration. They offer advantages such as easy scoring and direct relevance to specific job roles. However, they are susceptible to response manipulation and inaccuracies in self-perception, requiring careful administration and interpretation.

Task Performance Measures

Task performance measures assess personality through indirect and task-oriented tests, such as the Embedded Figures Test. These tests are designed to measure traits like field independence without direct self-reporting. However, they may involve ethical concerns due to their deceptive nature and often have questionable validity.

Reports by Others (360-Degree Feedback)

360-degree feedback gathers responses from an individual's colleagues at all levels, offering a broad perspective on the person's behavior and personality. While it benefits from multiple viewpoints, it faces challenges like potential bias, the necessity for raters to have close contact with the subject, and complex scoring processes.

Physiological Approaches

Physiological methods, such as measuring galvanic skin response, link physical reactions to psychological states, potentially providing objective measures of traits like stress. However, their applicability is limited, they can be manipulated through training and they raise ethical issues.

Situational Assessments

Situational assessments evaluate behavior through direct observation during task performance, providing a realistic measure of how individuals react in specific contexts. They are useful for identifying interpersonal skills and other job-relevant traits but require skilled observers and can be influenced by the subjects' awareness of being assessed.

Repertory Grid Technique

The Repertory Grid Technique, developed by George Kelly, uses comparisons among known elements to elicit personal constructs relevant to performance. It is valuable for in-depth personality analysis and counseling but is too time-consuming for routine selection processes and requires highly skilled practitioners.

Direct Observation of Behavior

Direct observation involves watching and noting behaviors in natural settings, offering rich, detailed data. This method is particularly effective with children in educational environments. Its main drawbacks are its time-consuming nature, potential observer bias, and the influence of the observer's presence on the subject's behavior.

The Interview

Despite being the most common assessment tool, interviews are often criticized for poor reliability and validity. Interviewers may form quick biases based on non-relevant criteria such as appearance. However, interviews are flexible and widely accepted by candidates.

The pleasures and pitfalls in trying to understand personality come from the very nature of humanity and fallibility. This reminds us that no matter what technique we employ, there will be risks surrounding our interpretations. These risks are associated with the three issues in the works—*bias, sabotage, and distortion*. The first, bias, comes from within the assessors themselves. Sabotage and distortion come largely from an interaction between the candidates and the assessors. Here is a more detailed explanation of what they mean:

Bias

It is impossible for any assessor to act like a robot and not bring aspects of their personality, attitudes, beliefs and prejudices to the assessment procedure. However, they can be aware of these factors and do everything possible to minimize their impact on their fellow human beings.

Sabotage

Candidates can sabotage the assessor's attempts to gain insights into their behavior, motives and underlying personality. Sabotage is always deliberate. It is most likely to occur when the person is defensive, protecting themselves, or simply suspicious of the tester's purposes and intentions toward them. Under these circumstances, the subject will ensure that the evaluator has no information about them that is of any value or credibility whatsoever.

Distortion

Distortion should not be confused with sabotage. In the latter case, no matter our methodology, the data is confounded and of no use. Distortion, however, may result in an assessor having useable and credible data because he or she is unaware that the candidate was attempting to mislead. Distortion may be intentional or unintentional. The first is most likely to occur in selection situations. The candidate develops (rightly or often wrongly) an impression of what the tester is looking for. He or she then modifies responses to fit this impression. Unintentional distortion can occur when the person lacks self-awareness.

Methods for Controlling/Minimizing Bias

Bias in personality assessment can arise from the reliance on the skills of interviewers, interpreters or observers, making methods like self-reports, interviews, projective techniques, repertory grids, direct observations, and situational assessments particularly susceptible. Techniques to minimize bias include:

- **Rigorous, Ongoing Training:** Enhancing the skills and knowledge of those conducting assessments to recognize and mitigate their biases.
- **Peer Review of Reports:** Having colleagues review reports to catch and correct biased interpretations.
- **Use of Computer-Generated Reports:** Where applicable, using technology to reduce human error and subjectivity in report generation.
- **Increasing Self-Awareness:** Encouraging assessors to understand and control their own prejudices, particularly in processes like interviews and situational assessments where stereotyping and the "halo/horns" effect can influence judgments.

Methods for Controlling/Minimizing Sabotage

Sabotage in assessments can stem from a subject's fear or defensiveness, especially if they suspect the motives behind the assessment. Strategies to reduce sabotage include:

- **Transparency About the Assessment's Purpose:** Clearly communicating the reasons for and the importance of the assessment.
- **Appropriate Method Selection:** Using the most suitable assessment methods for the intended purpose to avoid unnecessary resistance.
- **Clear Communication on Result Usage:** Being upfront about how the results will be utilized and ensuring they are used ethically and constructively.
- **Providing Honest Feedback:** Ensuring that candidates receive accurate feedback based on their assessment results, which helps in building trust.

Methods for Controlling/Minimizing Distortion

Distortion during assessments can be intentional or unintentional, driven by candidates' fear or suspicion about the process. Effective measures to minimize distortion include:

- **Open and Honest Briefing:** Clearly explaining the assessment's objectives and procedures to all participants.
- **Cross-Checking Results:** Where possible, verifying results through additional methods or sources to ensure accuracy.

- **Use of Response-Style Questions:** Incorporating questions that help identify and correct for personal biases or response styles in questionnaires.
- **Standardized Administration:** Applying consistent procedures across all assessments to ensure fairness and reliability.
- **Prompt Responses in Self-Reports:** Encouraging quick and spontaneous answers to reduce the opportunity for candidates to overthink or craft responses strategically.
- **Probing in Feedback Interviews:** Actively exploring and questioning responses during interviews to uncover deeper insights and clarify ambiguous answers.

Ethics in Personality Assessments

Using personality assessments in coaching offers deep insights but also demands a high level of ethical responsibility to benefit the client while avoiding potential harm and respecting professional boundaries.

- **Informed Consent:** Coaches must ensure clients fully understand and agree to the assessment by explaining its purpose, how the data will be used and any potential risks. This consent must be voluntary, and clients should have the freedom to withdraw it at any time.
- **Sensitive Feedback Delivery:** Given the personal nature of assessment results, coaches need to provide feedback with care, focusing on development and strengths rather than weaknesses. It's crucial to use empathetic language and allow clients time to process the information, being mindful of their verbal and non-verbal reactions.
- **Respecting Boundaries:** Assessments should be starting points for discussion rather than definitive conclusions about a client's character. Coaches should avoid making broad assumptions and refrain from pushing clients towards specific decisions, respecting the client's autonomy.
- **Data Privacy:** Protecting the confidentiality and integrity of assessment data is essential. Coaches should implement strict measures for data storage, encryption and destruction, ensuring clients are aware of how their information is used and have the option to opt out of any data sharing.
- **Cultural Sensitivity:** Assessments should be suitable for the client's cultural context, avoiding biases inherent in many standard tools. Coaches may need to adapt or select different assessments that are validated for the client's specific cultural background.
- **Avoiding Stereotypes:** It's important not to pigeonhole clients based on assessment results or demographic factors. Coaches should treat each client as an individual, using the assessment data to enhance personalized insights rather than enforce limiting labels.

- **Maintaining Objectivity:** Coaches should strive to remain neutral and objective, avoiding the influence of their own biases in interpreting and discussing results. It's important to use validated tools and present results transparently.
- **Emphasizing Continuous Development:** Recognizing that personality can evolve, coaches should not fixate on initial assessment outcomes. Periodic reassessments can provide updated insights, and coaches should remain attuned to any changes in the client's behavior that might suggest shifts in their traits or needs.

Ultimately, while personality assessments can be powerful tools in coaching, they must be used judiciously and ethically, always with the client's growth and well-being as the foremost priorities.

Adhering to ethical principles enhances the coaching process and builds trust. Coaches should continuously evaluate their personality assessment practices against ethical standards, obtain ongoing training and hold themselves accountable through coach certification requirements. When used ethically, personality assessments become powerful tools for illuminating clients' inner lives and activating their leadership potential.

Problems in Personality Assessments

Well-designed personality assessments, implemented by skilled practitioners, can boost public confidence in workplace personality testing. However, users and takers should be aware of certain pitfalls:

- **Spurious Validity:** Personality is inherently unique, challenging the standardization of its measurement. The Barnum Effect exemplifies spurious validity, where vague, general statements in reports can seem highly accurate to many individuals. This effect was famously demonstrated in studies where participants rated generic feedback as personally accurate, highlighting how easily people can perceive broad, non-specific feedback as uniquely applicable to them.
- **Pseudo-Scientific Measures:** Techniques like graphology, astrology and simplistic magazine quizzes often lack scientific reliability and validity. These methods, despite their popularity, do not withstand rigorous testing and can be misleading or even harmful. They fail to capture the complexity of personality traits and are thus discouraged for serious assessments.
- **Ipsative Questionnaires:** These questionnaires force respondents to choose the most and least accurate statements about themselves from a set, which theoretically reduces the potential for faking responses. However, studies indicate that ipsative formats are as susceptible to manipulation as normative questionnaires. Additionally, because these

assessments require trade-offs (scoring high on some traits necessitates scoring low on others), they cannot be directly compared to normative data. This forced-choice format creates a ranking of traits that reflects personal preference hierarchies rather than absolute trait levels, complicating the interpretation of results.

However, while personality assessments are valuable tools, their effectiveness depends on careful consideration of the design, implementation and inherent limitations of the methods used.

State vs. Trait Anxiety

Understanding the distinction between traits and states is crucial in the field of psychology, especially when considering their measurement and implications for behavior.

Traits vs. States: Traits are enduring characteristics that define a person's usual behavior, while states are transient and vary in duration and intensity. For example, **trait anxiety** refers to a general and consistent level of anxiety that a person typically exhibits, regardless of the situation. Conversely, **state anxiety** fluctuates and can spike in specific situations, such as experiencing stress during a traffic jam or while rushing to catch a train.

Several tools have been developed to differentiate between states and traits, such as the **State-Trait Anxiety Inventory (STAI-S)** by Spielberger (1984), which assesses how individuals feel in the moment vs. their general anxiety levels. Other instruments include the State-Trait Anger Scale, the Eight State Questionnaire and the Central State-Trait Kit. These instruments highlight that while many questionnaires measure trait anxiety, fewer assess state anxiety, which can significantly influence how responses are given based on current feelings.

The Big Five Theory: Another pivotal concept in understanding personality traits is the Big Five model,[10] which outlines five broad dimensions of personality:

- **Openness to Experience (O):** Reflects the degree of intellectual curiosity, creativity and preference for novelty and variety.
- **Conscientiousness (C):** Involves a spectrum from high levels of thoughtfulness, good impulse control and goal-directed behaviors, to less organized and more careless behaviors.
- **Extraversion (E):** Indicates an individual's sociability and tendency towards seeking stimulation in the company of others vs. being more reserved.
- **Agreeableness (A):** Describes a person's tendency to be compassionate and cooperative rather than suspicious and antagonistic towards others.
- **Neuroticism (N):** Identifies emotional stability and the tendency to experience unpleasant emotions easily.

These factors are considered traits because they are stable across different situations and are thought to have a genetic basis, possibly reflecting evolutionary adaptations. They are universally recognized across various cultures and provide a framework for understanding individual differences in personality. Distinguishing between traits and states is fundamental in personality psychology, helping to provide a more nuanced understanding of human behavior. Instruments designed to measure these aspects offer valuable insights, while the Big Five model organizes broad personality traits into a universally applicable framework, facilitating the study of how individuals vary in their typical patterns of thinking, feeling and behaving.

Interpreting the Validity and Utility of Personality Measurements

A test can be both standardized and reliable, yet still be unsuitable for certain assessments. For instance, when evaluating candidates for a senior management position using the criterion "Ability to Understand and Use Complex Numerical Data to Make Well-Reasoned Decisions," a test intended to measure advanced numerical reasoning might only include questions related to basic arithmetic computation. Although this test might demonstrate acceptable reliability, it fails to measure the specific capability it aims to assess. In essence, while it quantifies arithmetic skills accurately, it does not accurately predict proficiency in complex numerical reasoning.[11]

Therefore, when utilizing psychometric profiling, it is essential to understand the validity of assessments. Validity ensures that the tests genuinely measure the intended leadership qualities, which is critical for both identifying potential leaders and aiding their development.

Types of Validity

- Face Validity: Assesses whether the test appears relevant to leadership traits at a glance.
- Content Validity: Evaluates whether the test items specifically measure key leadership skills and competencies.
- Criterion-Related Validity: Measures how well a test's scores predict or relate to a specific outcome.
- Concurrent Validity: Measures how well test results align with current leadership performance.
- Predictive Validity: Determines the test's effectiveness in forecasting future leadership success.
- Construct Validity: Confirms that the test measures theoretical constructs important to leadership, such as strategic thinking and decision-making skills.

For leadership coaches, focusing on predictive and content validity is especially crucial. This focus ensures that the assessments not only predict future leadership effectiveness but also thoroughly evaluate essential leadership competencies. This strategic approach aids in choosing the best tools for assessing and developing effective leaders, ensuring that they are well-prepared to excel in their roles.

To select the most appropriate test, leadership coaches should:

- Review the Test's Validation Studies: Look for tests that provide clear, comprehensive validation studies that demonstrate reliability and validity in contexts similar to your needs.
- Evaluate Relevance: Ensure the test content aligns well with the specific leadership roles and competencies relevant to your organization.
- Consult with Peers: Seek advice from other experienced coaches who have used the tests and can provide firsthand insights into their effectiveness and applicability.
- Pilot the Test: Consider conducting a pilot study within your organization to see how well the test performs and whether it meets your developmental and assessment needs.

This understanding of validity types and strategic selection tips equips coaches and organizations to make educated decisions regarding the application of psychometric tests in leadership development programs, enhancing the effectiveness of their coaching initiatives.

Integrating Assessment Data into a Coaching Plan

Once personality assessments have been conducted and results delivered to the client, the next vital step is integrating the data into an actionable coaching plan. Assessment data provides unique insights into a client's attributes, tendencies and motivations. It can illuminate strengths to leverage and blind spots to develop when used effectively.

- Identifying strengths and growth areas: A foundational coaching practice is identifying strengths and growth opportunities in every assessment. Results indicating strong preferences or tendencies can have associated blind spots when overused in certain contexts. Alternatively, low scores that suggest weaknesses frequently carry inherent strengths if reframed. The coach should collaborate with the client to interpret results and brainstorm how strengths can be maximized and development areas addressed. Start by asking the client what they perceive as key takeaways, and build insight through supportive questioning.
- Selecting coaching interventions: After pinpointing key strengths and areas for growth, the coach can choose targeted interventions to

capitalize on or enhance these traits using leadership coaching with horses. For instance, if a client demonstrates notable assertiveness, the coaching may involve working with horses to refine their communication approach, teaching them to balance assertiveness with empathy and responsiveness, as horses react honestly and immediately to leadership styles. For those seeking greater connection, activities that encourage partnership and trust-building with horses can mirror the dynamics of workplace relationships, enhancing their sense of affiliation. Clients who need to boost their achievement drive might engage in goal-oriented exercises with horses, requiring clear planning and consistent effort to accomplish tasks. Coaches should articulate why specific horse-based interventions are selected, ensuring clients see the direct link between the exercises and their personal and professional development.

- Setting aligned development goals: Development goals in the coaching plan should directly align with and reinforce insights from assessment data. Having specific, measurable goals around targeted growth areas helps anchor coaching work and track progress. For example, if a client's assessment indicates difficulty receiving feedback, their goal could be to implement monthly check-ins with direct reports to gather candid input. Or an introverted client lacking self-promotion skills could set a goal for themselves to present at three leadership forums over the next year. Aligning goals and interventions is key for coaching effectiveness.

- Ongoing tracking and assessment: A single round of personality assessments provides only a snapshot, not an enduring portrait. People evolve over time. Coaches should periodically reassess clients using similar psychometric tools to gauge development in key areas and adjust coaching plans accordingly. Build in formal or informal assessment checkpoints every 4–6 months, and schedule reassessments to align with the conclusion of major coaching milestones. Compare results over time to quantify growth and add new goals based on emergent needs. Ongoing assessment is key for sustained development.

- Incorporating self-evaluation and observer feedback: While psychometric assessments provide helpful objective data, the subjective perspectives of clients themselves and those who work with them closely can add invaluable context. Schedule time to gather the client's self-perceptions before or after formal assessments. Be sure to explore any divergences between their self-view and formal results. The coach, upon the confirmation and agreement of the client, can also collect multirater feedback from the client's manager, peers, direct reports, etc., to incorporate observer perspectives into coaching. Utilize built-in features of assessment tools that allow observers to rate a client's displayed behaviors. Synthesize formal, self-report and observed data for a 360-degree view.

- Emphasizing concurrent change: The coaching process should emphasize a concurrent change in mindsets, behaviors and surrounding systems.

Personality assessments represent inherent traits and tendencies, but the client must take action to shift habits and demonstrate new behaviors consistently over time to realize change. Coaching should address links between a client's intrinsic attributes and their observable actions. Look for organizational norms or processes inhibiting demonstrated behavior change. The coach should take a systemic view, using assessment data to concurrently inform targeted development across intrinsic, behavioral and environmental domains.

- Adjusting approach based on readiness: Clients will differ in readiness to accept assessment results and act upon related coaching. Some may be enthused immediately, while others may resist or minimize tough feedback. Coaches must tailor their approach based on the client's stage of readiness for change. For reluctant clients, take time to process results, explore the pros and cons of changing, and empathetically understand their perspective. Avoid pushing forward with assessments or creating rigid coaching plans until the client has moved mentally from resistance to receptiveness. Adapt coaching pace and directiveness to the client's evolving readiness.

Personality assessments offer a profound opportunity to unlock self-awareness. However, their true power comes from how coaching integrates results into tailored development plans. With targeted goal-setting, appropriate interventions, organizational alignment and an adaptive coaching approach, assessment data can catalyze transformational and lasting growth for leadership clients.

Technology Trends in Personality Assessments

Technology has opened new possibilities for innovating both the delivery and analysis of personality assessments. Tech trends like mobile administration, gamification, instant reporting and AI integration are expanding access, engagement, depth of insights and predictive precision. While human interpretation remains essential, technology can enhance efficiency, personalization and the overall user experience.[12]

- Mobile assessments: Many assessments originally developed for pencil-and-paper are transitioning to mobile-friendly versions. Mobile personality tests allow for flexible administration, free from constraints like physical testing facilities. Test-takers can complete mobile assessments anytime, anywhere, via smartphones or tablets. For development programs, mobile assessments facilitate pre-work completion. Features like text reminders and intuitive interfaces aid convenience and follow-through. However, small screens may limit suitability for complex assessments. Mobile administration also requires stringent data security measures.

- Gamified assessments: Gamification applies game design elements to non-game contexts to increase engagement and motivation. Personality assessments incorporate gaming features such as avatars, points, badges, leaderboards and immersive scenarios. For example, an assessment may depict a character navigating workplace interactions, asking the test-taker what they would do next. Quiz questions may be embedded into an entertaining video game. While gamified assessments risk emphasizing entertainment over psychometrics, they can reduce perceptions of boredom/tedium. The competitive and social elements of gamification may also improve effort.

- Instant reporting: Many assessments now offer instant online access to results rather than delayed reports. Technology allows test-takers to receive automated scoring and analysis immediately after completing the assessment. Instant results enable test-takers to review their report independently and prepare for coaching conversations. For facilitators, this alleviates compilation and delivery efforts so they can focus on interpretation. However, poorly constructed narratives risk misinforming test-takers if taken as definitive without context. Nuanced coaching is still vital for proper understanding.

- AI-powered analysis: Artificial intelligence is enabling more sophisticated analysis of assessment data combined with more qualitative inputs, providing deeper personalization. Assessments increasingly integrate self-report data with AI analysis of facial expressions, body language, speech tone/patterns, and textual responses to identify subtle signals correlated with specific traits and tendencies. For example, vocal analysis software can detect emotions like anger or anxiety from speech far quicker than most humans can consciously perceive them. AI aims to surface hidden insights rather than taking self-reports at face value.

- Virtual reality (VR) simulations: VR environments are emerging as innovative options for observing behavioral responses linked to personality tendencies and leadership abilities. VR business simulations can mimic the ambiguity and pressure of real on-the-job scenarios to elicit behaviors in a controlled setting. For example, VR may simulate a crisis among agitated employees to assess a leader's approach to managing conflict. VR provides true experiential assessments vs. purely reflective self-reports. However, costs remain high, and limited empirical studies on VR assessment validity exist.

- Predictive analytics: Advances in AI, psychometrics and statistical modeling now allow predictive analytics using assessment data. Predictive talent analytics forecast candidates' likelihood of success in specific roles based on correlating assessment results with existing high performers' profiles. While still a nascent field requiring extensive validation, predictive personality analytics aims to convert assessment insights into statistically informed recruiting and development decisions. Privacy risks abound, however, if data usage becomes overly deterministic.

- Continuous reassessment: Many assessments are now moving from one-time events to continuous tracking of personalities and engagement via brief periodic pulse surveys. Technology enables low-burden reassessment using micro-surveys of just a few targeted questions sent via mobile devices. This facilitates monitoring trajectories over time rather than isolated snapshots. Continuous assessment allows for fluid, evolving personality profiles vs. fixed categorization. AI tailors reassessment question sets based on previous responses. However, survey fatigue remains a risk if not managed judiciously.

While technology cannot replace qualified coaches in delivering nuanced people insights, selected innovations can enrich and support the assessment process. The optimal approach harnesses tech-enabled efficiencies while retaining human insight. For example, mobile administration and instant reporting allow coaches to focus on interpretation rather than logistics, while AI-powered analysis surfaces new behavioral insights for exploration. Technology and humanity each have indispensable roles in evolving personality assessment capabilities.

Providing Feedback and Writing a Personality Assessment Report

In the context of coaching and personality assessment, feedback is a broad term to cover any discussion you have with someone about their profile. It is, therefore, wrong to assume that a "feedback interview" is somehow a separate event from any other interview. The only difference is that, unlike a normal interview, you will be sharing information with the candidate instead of merely asking questions.[13]

There are several reasons for giving feedback:

- Moral—we have asked someone to be open and self-revealing about themselves, and thus, we should be equally open with them.
- Ethical—a general code of practice requires always offering a candidate feedback.
- Concreteness—without discussing someone's profile, we cannot be certain what their responses mean to them. We want to explore and get concrete examples of their typical, everyday behaviors and preferences.

The Feedback Process

There are key stages and processes in giving feedback. These will apply no matter the assessment's purpose, i.e., the coach should adopt the same approach in the selection, career counseling, assessment of potential or the development of self-awareness. The stages include an introduction to the feedback, the feedback interview, and summarizing and conclusions.

Introduction to Feedback

The purpose of your introductory remarks is to:

- Outline the agenda
- Begin building a connection with the candidate
- Frame the context for the feedback session
- Assure the candidate about the confidentiality and use of their results
- Clarify the capabilities and limitations of the questionnaire
- Motivate the candidate to participate actively in the conversation

During the introduction, it's important to cover the following points:

- The report is based on a self-report questionnaire, reflecting the candidate's own perceptions of themselves.
- The questionnaire is not about right or wrong answers; it focuses on individual behavioral styles and preferences, not abilities.
- There are no "good" or "bad" profiles, though some may align better with specific roles.
- While not perfect, the questionnaire typically provides a reliable reflection of how people see themselves.
- The results are comparative, meaning the candidate's responses are benchmarked against those from a broader group, such as managers, graduates, or sales professionals.
- Explain how the questionnaire is integrated into broader selection and development processes, emphasizing that it is just one component.
- Discuss the confidentiality of the data and who will have access to it.
- Highlight the importance of dialogue during the feedback session, aiming for a balanced discussion with equal input from both sides.
- Encourage any questions they might have and ensure their comfort moving forward.
- Obtain their consent to proceed with the process.

The Feedback

While there is no one correct way of providing feedback, these activities should be included:

- Describe the scope of the questionnaire.
- Proceed logically—avoid jumping around the profile.
- Mix direct feedback with questions—e.g., "You said that you enjoy creative problem solving, tell more about that" vs. "Talk a little about your typical approach to solving problems."

- Probe and follow up—get concrete examples where possible. Try not to ask for an example repeatedly. Rather, ask open-ended questions, such as "How might I notice that in your day-to-day work?"
- Avoid saying, "You ARE..." They might not be. It is better to say, "From how you have described yourself, it appears that..."
- Summarize at the end of each section.
- Make sure they do at least 50% of the talking.
- Don't give them the profile chart.

Summarizing and Concluding

- Bring things to a close by saying, "We seem to have agreed, then, that..."
- Provide a conclusion. This might be action planning in the case of a development interview or the case of a selection setting, a reinforcement of what happens next.

General Report-Writing Guidelines

These guidelines are applicable to virtually any report that discusses an individual's profile, with additional specific instructions provided for candidate or third-party reports and those within different contexts.

Introduction:

- Clearly state the nature and objectives of the assessment.
- Detail what the assessment measures and describe its structure.
- Explain the norms used, including their selection rationale.
- Acknowledge the limitations of self-report personality assessments, emphasizing their potential fallibility.
- Mention any additional data used to support conclusions, such as data from interviews, job performance reviews, ability tests, and interest inventories.

Body of the report:

- Tailor the style and language to suit the intended audience.
- Organize the report with meaningful headings, potentially based on assessment criteria.
- Focus on describing behavioral outcomes and preferences rather than merely presenting scale scores.
- Interpret scale scores with precision, avoiding exaggeration or avoidance of difficult topics.
- Draw connections between relevant personality dimensions.
- Communicate findings in clear, behavioral terms that are easy to understand.

- Steer clear of speculative or clinical interpretations that lack evidence.
- Maintain an objective tone, refraining from imposing personal biases.
- Incorporate and integrate data from other sources when available.
- Reflect upon the feedback interview content rather than merely reiterating initial interpretations.
- Discuss all reviewed data openly in the report, ensuring transparency.

Conclusions:

- Draw valid conclusions that logically stem from the body of the report.
- Avoid over-stating the reliability or accuracy of the personality assessment tools used.
- Address any inconsistencies or concerns that arise during the assessment process.
- Provide a balanced view of the individual's potential strengths and limitations, ensuring that no single aspect is disproportionately highlighted.

Specific Report-Writing Guidelines

Reports for third parties:

- Do not include information that has not been shared with the candidate.
- Include a clear reminder about confidentiality and use, such as time scales, specific purpose of the report and who should have access to the report.

Reports for candidates:

- Write in the second person.
- Use positive language without evading more difficult areas.
- Take the context for the individual into account, i.e., development, counseling, etc.
- Be sure to address developmental issues and options.
- Offer opportunities for further discussion.

Selection reports:

- Define criteria and competencies assessed.
- Highlight how the personality assessment tool relates to these criteria.
- Do not over-state the relationship between personality traits and job performance.
- Emphasize that the report is NOT to be used on its own for final decision.

Developmental reports (personal, career, etc.):

- Relate behaviors to meaningful situations—career choice.
- Identify the need for further information—abilities, interests and resources.
- Offer developmental suggestions where appropriate.

The psychometric assessment process uncovers invaluable insights into the mental and emotional drivers underlying leadership behaviors and developmental needs. Paired with the physiological insights revealed through biofeedback and experiential horse activities, coaches gain an enriched 360-degree perspective. HRV patterns signaling emotional regulation capacities can be explored in relation to assessing personality dimensions, cognitive capacities, motivational tendencies and more. This fusion of psychological and biofeedback data empowers integrated analysis, elevating self-awareness regarding innate reactiveness, reflexive habits and untapped potential. Coaches can then target personalized development plans to leverage individuals' strengths while addressing blind spots and setting aligned goals. Additional horse interactions focused on practicing emotional centering skills can reinforce learning, with biofeedback guiding technique effectiveness. The synergy between mental, emotional and physiological realms is key to conscious, empowered leadership actualization. While there are many options available regarding psychometric profiling, as this chapter illustrates, a handful typically work best in conjunction with biofeedback. In the next chapter, we begin to weave all these elements together.

Notes

1 Borsboom, D., & Molenaar, D. (2015). Psychometrics. In J. D. Wright (Ed.), *International encyclopedia of the social & behavioral sciences* (2nd ed.) (pp. 418–422). Elsevier.
2 Borghans, L., Duckworth, A. L., Heckman, J. J., & ter Weel, B. (2008). The economics and psychology of personality traits. *The Journal of Human Resources*, 43 (4), 972–1059. www.jstor.org/stable/40057376.
3 Stein, R., Swan, A. B., & Eureka College. (2019). Evaluating the validity of Myers-Briggs Type Indicator theory: A teaching tool and window into intuitive psychology. *Social and Personality Psychology Compass*, 13(2), e12434. https://doi.org/10.1111/spc3.12434.
4 Karimi, S., Ahmadi Malek, F., Yaghoubi Farani, A., & Liobikienė, G. (2023). The role of transformational leadership in developing innovative work behaviors: The mediating role of employees' psychological capital. *Sustainability*, 15(2), 1267. https://doi.org/10.3390/su15021267.
5 Küssner, M. B. (2017). Eysenck's theory of personality and the role of background music in cognitive task performance: A mini-review of conflicting findings and a new perspective. *Frontiers in Psychology*, 8, 1991. https://doi.org/10.3389/fpsyg.2017.01991.
6 MacDonald, K. B. (1988). *Social and personality development: An evolutionary synthesis.* SpringerLink. https://link.springer.com/book/10.1007/978-1-4757-0292-7.

 7 Wright, A. G. C. (2011). Qualitative and quantitative distinctions in personality disorder. *Journal of Personality Assessment*, 93(4), 370–379. https://doi.org/10.1080/00223891.2011.577477.

 8 American Psychological Association. (2003, July/August). Personality changes for the better with age. *Monitor on Psychology*, 34(7), 14. www.apa.org/monitor/julaug03/personality.

 9 Lapsley, D., & Ste, P. C. (2012). *Id, ego, and superego*. University of Notre Dame. https://doi.org/10.1016/B978-0-12-375000-6.00199-3.

10 Soto, C. J. (2018). Big Five personality traits. In M. H. Bornstein (Ed.), *The Sage encyclopedia of lifespan human development* (pp. 240–241). Sage Publications.

11 Paunonen, S. V. (1984). Optimizing the validity of personality assessments: The importance of aggregation and item content. *Journal of Research in Personality*, 18(4), 411–431. https://doi.org/10.1016/0092-6566(84)90001-1.

12 Ihsan, Z., & Furnham, A. (2018). The new technologies in personality assessment: A review. *Consulting Psychology Journal: Practice and Research*, 70(2). https://doi.org/10.1037/cpb0000106.

13 Del Giudice, M. J., Yanovsky, B. I., & Finn, S. E. (2014). Personality assessment and feedback practices among executive coaches: In search of a paradigm. *Consulting Psychology Journal: Practice and Research*, 66(3), 155–172. https://doi.org/10.1037/cpb0000007.

Chapter 4

The Convergence of Equine Wisdom, Psychometric Insights and Biofeedback in Leadership

This chapter explores the innovative methodology of combining the three complementary modalities outlined in this book—equine-assisted learning, psychometric assessments and biofeedback technology—to take leadership training to a new level of insight and proficiency. The outcome of converging these three methods of learning results in a holistic coaching and leadership experience. Horse interactions offer a dynamic environment for concrete skill-building, psychometric insights provide an empirical map of inner traits and tendencies, and biofeedback lends real-time data to decode stress responses and emotional states. The synergy of these elements sets the stage for profound transformation, from cultivating self-awareness to developing emotional intelligence and authentic leadership capabilities.

Further, this chapter will illustrate how this integrated approach comes to life during coaching sessions, and explore how activities with horses, informed by psychometric profiles and biofeedback data, can hone communication skills, build stress resilience, and foster authentic, values-driven leadership. The chapter will also outline how leaders can transfer insights from this experiential approach into daily leadership practice and long-term development.

The Synergy of Horses, Psychometrics and Biofeedback

The true power of this development methodology lies in the synergistic integration of three modalities into one arena, bringing interactive, real-time responses from horses, a leader's personality traits, cognitive styles and behavioral tendencies, and their physiological responses to stress and tension into one cohesive learning environment.

While each modality offers distinct value, the combination catalyzes exponential leadership growth. This holistic methodology, rooted in scientific validity, yet humanized through sentient interactions, unlocks transformative development pathways. And integrating all three perspectives results in multidimensional development.

Incorporating horses, psychology and technology enables leadership development that integrates mind, body and relationships. This holistic

DOI: 10.4324/9781032683843-5

framework crafted from complementary disciplines culminates in transformative growth rooted in scientific rigor, experiential practice and self-awareness.

The Equestrian Mirror: Reflecting and Guiding Leadership Qualities

As stated in earlier chapters, horses serve as mirrors reflecting leadership behaviors and interpersonal tendencies. If a leader is unfocused, then the horse will become unfocused, too. Coaches can observe if leaders attempt to understand why a horse may be reacting in an odd way vs. becoming impatient or shutting down emotionally. These responses reveal how challenges, mistakes and miscommunications are processed.

Horses also respond literally to the present moment. A leader preoccupied with past failures or future worries will struggle to gain cooperation.[1] Horses demand full attentiveness to the task at hand. This mindful presence is immediately revealed when a leader's thinking strays from the immediate interaction. Thus, horses provide concrete feedback about focus, calibration and consistency—key leadership capacities. Each exercise offers opportunities to discover unconscious dynamics through the horse's responses, responses that are mirroring our inner thoughts and feelings.

Opportunities to practice reading different horse personalities also build interpretive skills. Like humans, each horse has a distinct temperament and history, shaping their responses. Nervous horses provide lessons in staying grounded when faced with others' anxiety. Stoic horses require assertiveness and motivation skills to elicit engagement. Naturally playful horses help leaders connect with lightness during tense times.[2] Learning to attune to each horse's unique nature parallels the discernment required in human relationships. Equine-assisted leadership development leverages horses' innate authenticity, sensitivity and embodiment of presence. As sentient beings, horses provide pure experiential learning—no books or theories, just immediate feedback. The awareness gained from reading their responses becomes an embodied tool leaders carry forward. This supports the metacognitive capacity, empathy and connection skills that underpin impactful leadership. Horses model how to distill truth from the silent language of being.

Biofeedback: The Physiological Compass for Emotional Regulation

Biofeedback sensors offer a complementary layer of concrete data to enhance the decoding of equine responses. Heart rate variability (HRV) and skin conductivity provide physiological insights into emotional reactions during interactions. For instance, a leader may feel perplexed when a horse ignores their commands. The biofeedback sensors reveal high-stress responses and anxiety underlying the interaction. This enables a deeper linkage between embodied states, behaviors and outcomes. Biofeedback helps strengthen leaders' capacity to self-regulate during challenges with the horses. Portable neurofeedback devices allow real-time monitoring of brainwave activity related to focus and calmness.[3] As leaders practice maintaining optimal brain states while interacting with the horses, their ability to stay regulated during interpersonal stress is reinforced. This integration of body and mind supports the meta-cognitive awareness essential to interpret situations accurately.

Importantly, biofeedback is woven into activities with intentionality. For instance, a leader first establishes a calm HRV baseline. They then perform progressively more challenging tasks with the horse while observing their HRV patterns. Coaches help interpret the biological signals about experiences with the horse, revealing connections between thoughts, feelings and physiology. Over repeated sessions, leaders build awareness of their stress triggers, learn to regulate physiological reactions and integrate mind-body intelligence. Biofeedback unlocks a powerful reflective portal into leaders' inner landscapes. The technology renders biology transparent, helping integrate the body's wisdom with emotional and cognitive insight. This accelerates self-understanding and the development of agile, mindful, resonant leadership. Cultivating self-awareness and managing stress responses leads to more conscious, productive and ethical leadership.

Developing Emotional Intelligence and Authentic Leadership

Emotional intelligence and authentic leadership are qualities highly prized in the realm of effective leadership. Relationships are the lifeblood of effective leadership. Emotional intelligence, the ability to understand and manage emotions in ourselves and others, is essential for ethical, compassionate and motivating leadership. Authenticity—leading in alignment with one's true values and purpose—engenders trust and inspires engagement. Equine-assisted activities offer a fertile training ground for cultivating these relationship-based leadership competencies. Horses demand leaders operate with emotional intelligence as they immediately react to inauthentic gestures or discordant emotions.[4] Unlike humans, horses do not judge, but their honest feedback exposes when leaders are not acting with integrity regarding their true feelings and intentions. This compels leaders to align their emotions and behaviors to establish trust and cooperation with the horse.

Furthermore, horses have distinct personalities and motivations, just like people. So, leaders must practice flexing their leadership style to influence each horse based on its unique nature. For example, apprehensive horses require patience and calm authority, while independent horses respond to confident guidance. Adapting in this way expands emotional intelligence, as self- and social awareness are strengthened to meet the needs of each horse.

Cultivating presence and internal calm are essential to lead effectively. This demands tuning into emotional and physiological states moment-to-moment—skills enabling agile situational leadership in human relationships.

Cultivating self-awareness and emotional intelligence provides the foundation for impactful leadership rooted in authenticity and compassion. Equine activities offer a fertile environment to strengthen these intrapersonal and interpersonal skills through experiential learning. This section will explore sample exercises integrating horse interactions with biofeedback data to reveal blind spots, accelerate self-understanding and expand emotional capacity.

A foundational exercise involves observing one's physiological stress patterns when encountering novel stimuli. For instance, a leader unfamiliar with horses will approach and then be asked to groom the horse while wearing a HRV sensor. The biofeedback reveals rising stress response—quickened heart rate, diminished HRV amplitude—during first contact vs. gradual arousal regulation as comfort builds. This exposes ingrained neurological response patterns to uncertainty. The leader reflects on how this manifests at work, perhaps in impatience with unclear tasks or avoiding stakeholder interactions outside their comfort zone. With coaching, the leader can practice paced breathing to calm physiological arousal and sustain regulated presence during unfamiliar leadership scenarios.

Another potent exercise utilizes video review. A leader performs activities like leading a horse over obstacles while being recorded. Observing their body language and facial expressions that betray frustration, fear or impatience provides a window into unconscious emotional dynamics and typical reactions. Integrating this feedback into self-narrative creates openings for increased self-acceptance, cognitive reframing of challenges and practicing more adaptive physiological regulation. Over repeated viewings, the visual-soma-sensory feedback loop enables leaders to reset unproductive response patterns and act from emotional intelligence.

Equine activities also build social awareness and empathy. Leaders take turns leading a horse through a maze in partner exercises without speaking or physically contacting their partner. This requires observing micro-expressions and bodily cues to intuit directions. Sensors tracking heart rate or skin conductance provide biofeedback on physiological activation, revealing when leaders become frustrated or remain calm and attentive. This exercise develops patience, non-verbal attunement, and understanding of different thinking styles when collaborating—capacities directly applicable to team leadership. Debriefs focus on discussing emotional responses and extracting lessons around reading non-verbal cues, communicating with care, and regulating stress for optimal partnership.

Communication Skills and Assertiveness

Non-verbal communication forms the foundation of leadership presence and influence. Research shows that 93% of human communication occurs through non-verbal cues, including body language, facial expressions, vocal tonality, and energy.[5] Equine activities offer a masterclass in honing these silent leadership skills. With no verbal language between species, horses respond entirely to the non-verbal messages a leader projects. This heightens leaders' awareness of how their embodied presence and behaviors impact relationships. For instance, horses mirror back incongruences between a leader's words and body language. Speaking calmly while feeling anxious yields reactions of unease from the horse. This vividly showcases the power of non-verbal communication and helps leaders practice aligning their gestures, posture and tone with intentionality.[6] Body language signaling confidence while maintaining inner calm elicits the horse's attention and trust. Exercises aimed at influencing horses through energy and intention highlight how humans unconsciously transmit emotions. Practicing projecting feelings of joy or calm without physical cues or language develops a leader's energetic presence. According to Roberts (1996), a leader's effectiveness lies in their ability to exert willful intention through focused emotion. Learning to direct positive emotional states consciously builds a charismatic presence.[7]

Boundary-setting is also central to non-verbal leadership authority. Horses respond to clear spatial boundaries and calm assertiveness.[8] Leaders must practice maintaining composure while insisting the horse comply with directions. This builds confidence in exerting influence balanced with compassion. Blending boundary clarity with empathetic leadership presence results in horses mirroring focus, trust and followership. Biofeedback aids conscious mastery of non-verbal skills by making the physical manifestations of emotions visible. Sensors provide feedback on how the body is affected by practicing influencing horses through energy and intention. Leaders can observe how visualizing success creates physiological coherence. This helps anchor positive emotional states through embodied self-awareness. Monitoring brainwaves with EEG neurofeedback exposes how mental focus impacts leadership presence. As leaders learn to sustain attentional states that manifest as alpha and theta brainwave patterns, horses respond positively to their enhanced mindfulness and confidence. Integrating this mind-body feedback helps leaders apply non-verbal communication for relationship-building.

Equine activities distill leadership down to its purest non-verbal essence. Words disappear as horses respond only to what energy communicates. Through this embodied practice, leaders tune into their presence and refine awareness of how each non-verbal signal impacts others. Compassionate leadership emerges from exercising these skills in service of cooperative relationships with horses.

Integrating biofeedback into equine leadership training brings conscious awareness to the embodied foundations of communication. Noticing how emotions, thoughts and language intersect builds coherence. The technology also develops empathy and attunement to others' non-verbal signals. This results in resonant, values-based leaders who communicate with integrity, compassion and influence.

Experiential Learning and Leadership Development

Experiential learning theory emphasizes the importance of active experience, reflection and application for transformational growth. Equine-assisted leadership activities use this process through hands-on experiences that challenge leaders to test and refine their skills in an immediately responsive environment. Interacting with and influencing 1000-pound animals serves as a masterclass in self-awareness, relationship-building, non-verbal communication, and stress management. With their hypervigilance and lack of pretense, horses provide instant, honest feedback by mirroring leaders' emotions and actions back to them.[9] If a leader feels confident, but is betraying underlying anxiety through subtle physical cues, the horse will respond skittishly and refuse to cooperate. This requires slowing down to align internal states with outward behavior authentically. Processing what emotions, thoughts and physical tensions betray leadership presence builds self-awareness. Repeating activities with different horses provides opportunities to apply insights across various relationship dynamics. For example, leaders may practice harnessing intentions to direct a compliant horse and adjust their energy to motivate a resistant horse. Through these experiential iterations, approach flexibility and empathy develop. Each interaction with a horse serves as a microcosm for exploring and honing leadership skills.

Horses compel leaders to be fully embodied and attuned to the present interaction.[10] As prey animals, horses respond immediately to threats perceived in the leader's state of being. Therefore, leaders cultivate focus and regulation skills by sustaining a mindful, positive presence during equine activities. This transfers directly to managing stress and leading consciously amid workplace demands. Equine-assisted development leverages challenge, repetition, reflection and embodiment principles to transform leadership ability. Activities amplify workplace dynamics in visceral ways, eliciting responses that expose blind spots. Integration is strengthened as insights arise from felt experience. Through ongoing practice and application of relationship skills with horses, leaders become more agile, compassionate and authentic.

Case Studies of Transformational Leadership Journeys

While conceptual models provide a helpful structure, real-world examples bring a methodology to life. Below are case studies exemplifying the transformative impacts of this integrated equine-assisted leadership coaching approach grounded in biofeedback and psychological assessments.

Marissa S., a Director of Operations, is a driven and high-achieving individual who initially faced challenges in forming connections with her team.

Assessments indicated that she tended to be analytical and reserved in her relationships. However, during coaching sessions involving horses, a different side of Marissa emerged, displaying strong empathy and charisma. This experience with the horses revealed her natural ability to relate to others, which was then harnessed to enhance her leadership presence. With targeted guidance, Marissa learned to project more care and vulnerability. Biofeedback sessions confirmed that these changes positively affected her physiology, creating a more coherent state. Over the course of six months, feedback from 360-degree reviews showed significant improvement, as Marissa continued to develop her skills in being personable, articulate and empowering.

James R., an emerging entrepreneur, needed to develop mature, strategic leadership to scale his business. Psychometrics highlighted a tendency for impulsivity and self-doubt. Observations confirmed James initially lacked presence with the horses, reflecting low self-efficacy. However, James demonstrated strong intuition in reading the horses' needs. This strength was leveraged in coaching to build confidence and situational awareness. With biofeedback training, James learned to regulate emotional responses and access inner calm. His leadership aligned with his essence, leading to bold, mindful decision-making.

Eva L., a high-potential technical expert, presented with a cognitive leadership style and wanted to advance into people leadership. Assessments showed limited natural extroversion and a distrust of emotions. Yet Eva demonstrated compassion for the horses. With guidance to embrace this emotional capacity, Eva practiced projecting care and vulnerability with the horses. Coaching helped translate these skills into more resonant team leadership. Eva integrated mindfulness through biofeedback to sustain coherence during interactions. Her inventive technical leadership gained an accessible, inspirational human dimension.

Cross-case patterns demonstrate how this methodology allows leaders to leverage natural strengths revealed through equine interactions while addressing countervailing tendencies identified in psychological instruments. Integrating biofeedback accelerates personalized growth by making patterns tangible. The result is an integrated leadership presence sourced from aligning potential with the purpose of empowered impact.

Enhancing Team Dynamics Through Group Equine Sessions

Shared horse activities can reveal team dynamics and develop collective leadership capabilities. Biofeedback monitors each member's stress responses, making patterns visible. Debriefs facilitate discussing how collaboration, attention to detail, risk-taking and bigger-picture thinking emerged. This maximizes strengths while building self-awareness to manage reactive tendencies and leads to shared purpose. Follow-up coaching can reinforce integration.

Additionally, paired grounding exercises where team members seek to calm down and synchronize with a horse provide biofeedback on shared physiological states. When coherence occurs, the horse responds through proximity and lowered stress signals. This builds trust and the capacity to regulate under pressure collectively. Herd-oriented animals like horses can model the attributes of high-performing teams, including attunement, purposeful collaboration and resilience. Equine therapy provides opportunities to practice and improve dysfunctional team dynamics through immediate experiential feedback. Integrating biofeedback accelerates awareness of individual and collective social-emotional states to strengthen bonding.

Cultivating Practical Skills

Effective, values-based leadership relies on clear communication and the ability to find connection and understanding with others. Equine activities offer opportunities to practice and refine verbal and non-verbal communication skills. Integrating biofeedback accelerates awareness of how one's presence, physiology and energy impact relationships. Foundational skills include using assertive yet compassionate verbal tones and body language to guide a horse through tasks. Leaders wear biofeedback sensors that monitor inner states like heart rate, skin conductance or muscle tension. This concrete feedback reveals how tones of voice and physical gestures communicate intentions and shape responses. With coaching, leaders strengthen skills for conveying clarity, establishing boundaries, and building cooperation through mindful language and presence. As adaptive communication patterns integrate, leaders observe horses responding with increased focus and trust. What is embodied physically and energetically transmits leadership qualities.

Another exercise involves practicing motivating language. Leaders are tasked with being highly engaging, using voice modulation and non-verbal cues to invite a reticent horse to approach. Biofeedback sensors show how enthusiasm manifests physiologically through activating the sympathetic nervous system. Leaders learn to sustain this energetic state with guidance while communicating vision and possibility. This dynamic communication training translates directly into inspiring teams towards shared goals, yet it retains the service orientation of regulating arousal for cooperative relationships as opposed to manipulation. As philosopher Krishnamurti noted, "Right communication comes into being only when there is silence in your mind" (1956).[11]

Integrating Skills into Daily Leadership Practice

Leaders need methods to integrate insights into leadership routines for learning transfers from training to sustainable practice. Ongoing biofeedback practice and reflection help embody new behavioral patterns and self-regulation skills. Coaches prescribe protocols aligned to each leader's growth goals. For communicators working to improve presence, daily HRV training could include reviewing physiological patterns during past challenging interactions to understand reactivity and practice regulating responses through paced breathing. Breathing exercises are recommended before and during high-stakes meetings to sustain coherence. Leaders seeking more inspirational and engaging styles can use neurofeedback recordings during creative thinking or team presentations. Noticing brain patterns provides tangible feedback to understand when they access optimal flow states. With practice sustaining the ideal ratios of alpha, beta and theta waves, presence and influence organically expand. Supporting leaders in establishing mindfulness habits fosters embodiment. Using smartwatch-based pulse sensors to track daily HRV patterns provides insight into subjective well-being and emotional regulation capacity.[12] Over time, noticing optimal and suboptimal states reinforces the motivators and conditions for peak leadership. Additionally, brief diary or audio journaling about observed situational responses, communication patterns and stress triggers can help leaders integrate insights. Encapsulating learning evolves understanding from fleeting experiences to solidified self-knowledge, ensuring development transfers from the equine arena to daily leadership.

Developing Emotional Agility in Leadership

Emotional agility, the ability to process and channel emotions in a healthy and adaptive way, is essential for effective leadership. It enables leaders to encounter both positive and negative emotions with an attitude of openness, mindfulness and resilience. This adaptive capability allows for a flexible response to challenges, rather than a rigid, reactive one.[13]

Incorporating psychometric profiling into leadership development programs enriches the understanding of a leader's emotional and cognitive patterns. By assessing individual psychological attributes and emotional competencies, coaches can personalize the approach to each leader's unique profile. This profiling, when combined with equine activities and biofeedback training, creates a multifaceted experiential platform for leaders to enhance their emotional agility.

During equine-assisted activities, leaders are encouraged to reflect on work situations that invoke strong emotions such as anger or anxiety. In this reflective practice, they recreate these emotional states while engaging with a horse, which serves as a sensitive barometer for the leader's internal emotional landscape. Monitoring their physiological responses through biofeedback sensors, leaders learn to apply self-regulation techniques, like paced breathing, to achieve a state of coherence.

The immediate and honest feedback from the horse compels leaders to fine-tune their emotional awareness and control, fostering a heightened sense of emotional intelligence. Over time, such interactions help in developing a "muscle memory" for navigating emotional triggers with regulated, value-aligned responses.

Furthermore, leaders engage in exercises that focus on cultivating positive emotional states. They identify work relationships that are invigorating and seek to emulate those feelings of positivity in interactions with the horses. HRV training is used to maintain a state of physiological coherence, aligning with feelings of gratitude and appreciation.[14] This practice not only bolsters the ability to manage stress but also refines the leader's capacity to invoke and sustain positive emotions.

Neurofeedback is another tool used in these exercises, where leaders observe the impact of different cognitive strategies on their brainwave patterns. These patterns are indicative of resilience and a sense of empowerment. As leaders integrate these cognitive strategies into their behavior, they witness a tangible growth in their emotional agility.

Merging psychometric profiling, equine-assisted activities and biofeedback within the leadership coaching framework, leaders can develop a profound mastery over their emotional dexterity, intelligence and resilience. This holistic approach ensures that leaders are not only reacting to their environments but also proactively cultivating an emotionally agile leadership style.

Data-Driven Personal Development Strategies

The integration of psychometric assessments and biofeedback results enables a data-driven approach to mapping leaders' strengths and development areas and tailoring growth plans accordingly. Psychological instruments provide empirical insights into personality traits, thinking styles, motivations and behavioral tendencies. Biofeedback offers concrete data on stress reactivity, emotional states and self-regulation capacity. This level of precision allows coaches to design development strategies targeting the specific areas leaders need to stretch to reach the next level of effectiveness. Programs can include communication training to strengthen natural extroversion, mindfulness practices to improve resilience, or role-play exercises to develop confidence. Ongoing biofeedback practice helps leaders integrate changes through immediate feedback on responses to new behaviors. For example, assertive language that produces excessive physiological arousal would signal more calibration is needed to align boldness with inner coherence. Data ensures development is embodied for maximal translation to leadership practice.

Tools for Continuous Leadership Growth

Sustainable change requires consistent reinforcement. Leaders can employ biofeedback as part of an ongoing development regimen. Ubiquitous technology like smartwatches makes tracking HRV accessible outside train-ing facilities.[15] Monitoring daily HRV provides insight into lifestyle factors that fuel resilience and productivity. This empowers leaders to make choices aligned with peak performance. Leaders can also integrate breathing and mindfulness exercises to self-generate states of coherence. Biofeedback apps like Resonance provide training sequences and audio guidance grounded in neuroscience research.[16] Daily practice builds emotional regulation skills over time. Reflective practices like leadership journaling allow continued integra-tion of development insights. Writing or audio recording leadership experi-ences, key learnings and emotions provides metacognitive processing and clarity. This cements the translation of training into tangible growth and capability expansion. Combined, these tools and techniques sustain leader-ship development as a lifelong endeavor centered on maximizing potential through mindful, data-driven self-mastery practices.

Designing Effective Leadership Coaching Programs

To enhance the effectiveness of leadership development, the comprehensive framework suggested in this book can be implemented to leverage the inte-gration of psychometrics, biofeedback and equine-assisted coaching. The framework builds upon the foundational steps outlined below:

1 **Leadership Profiling:** A thorough psychometric assessment to understand the leader's personality, strengths and areas for development.
2 **Biofeedback:** Leaders are connected to biofeedback data-tracking tools to establish a baseline and measure the daily data and how they change based on the work stimuli.
3 **Coaching Sessions with Horses:** During the coaching session, leaders are again connected to a biofeedback tracker to monitor their phy-siological responses. This tracker provides real-time data on bodily metrics. With this valuable information, coaches can tailor the equine-assisted coaching sessions to each leader's psychometric and biometric profiles.
4 **Biofeedback-Informed Coaching Strategies:** Following the biofeedback review and coaching sessions with horses, the coaching process continues by integrating biofeedback data monitoring with coaching strategies. This involves tailoring interventions to enhance the leader's self-regulation and resilience based on their physiological responses.
5 **Reflection and Application:** Reflective practices after each coaching ses-sion prompt leaders to integrate insights from psychometrics, biofeed-back and equine-assisted coaching into their leadership approach. Furthermore, support should be provided to the leader in developing action plans to apply newfound knowledge and skills in their professional context, fostering ongoing growth and development.

Leadership Profiling

Leadership profiling can be defined as an interdisciplinary assessment approach that combines the analytical rigor of forensic methodologies, traditionally utilized in criminal profiling, with the nuanced understanding of validated psychometric tools and frameworks from organizational psychology. It represents a groundbreaking methodological framework aimed to substantially further the understanding of the intricate tapestry of multidimensional attributes, behaviors, competencies and potentialities underlying leadership excellence and trajectories across the career lifespan.

Specifically, leadership profiling comprehensively integrates robust psychometric testing with in-depth behavioral pattern analysis of a leader's career progression, decision-making watersheds, team-building capabilities, communication styles and responses to uncertainty. This enables the construction of integrated psychometric-behavioral profiles for talent screening and targeted development interventions. Consequently, forensic leadership profiling allows organizations to implement an empirically based architecture for identifying, nurturing and predictively modeling the key differentiators of high-potential talent while mitigating risks of misjudgments that lead to placing wrong leaders in pivotal roles.

The analytical procedure entails meticulously mapping the career inflection points, progression speed, lateral moves, intrinsic motivators, skills acquisition pacing, leadership style adaptiveness and emotional intelligence trajectory. Given the leader's current profile, this modeling uses Bayesian analytics, a method of statistical inference, to determine the probability of successful vertical transition. In addition, the forensic profiling lens elucidates how leaders confront uncertainty, adapt to turbulence, realign team priorities and maintain resilience during career crucibles. These behavioral insights feed into machine learning algorithms that categorize and rank high-potential leaders based on statistical commonalities with existing top talent.

Altogether, implementing leadership profiling ushers organizations into a new era of leadership coaching and analytics, providing a multidimensional decision framework for development and recruiting as well as tailored acceleration of future senior leadership. This allows a profound, predictive, scientifically grounded understanding of leadership excellence's cognitive, emotional, and experiential foundations.

Key characteristics of leadership profiling (LP):

1 BEHAVIORAL PATTERN ANALYSIS

- LP involves the study of behavioral patterns within leadership contexts, mirroring the precision with which crime profilers examine behaviors and motives in criminal investigations.

2 PSYCHOLOGICAL ATTRIBUTE MEASUREMENT

- It leverages psychometric tools to measure and evaluate psychological attributes such as personality traits, cognitive abilities and behavioral tendencies that are significant for effective leadership.

3 PREDICTIVE MODELING

- LP uses predictive modeling to anticipate leadership success and identify potential challenges, drawing on data-driven insights to inform leadership selection, development and succession planning.

4 ETHICAL AND DECISION-MAKING ANALYSIS

- Ethical considerations and decision-making processes are scrutinized, akin to forensic evaluations, to assess a leader's judgment, integrity and moral reasoning in complex situations.

5 CRISIS AND CONFLICT-MANAGEMENT EVALUATION

- The method includes simulating crisis scenarios and conflicts to evaluate a leader's response under pressure, providing insights into their resilience, resourcefulness and strategic thinking.

6 INTEGRATION OF ORGANIZATIONAL DATA

- LP integrates analytical techniques with organizational data, such as performance metrics and team dynamics, to construct a comprehensive profile of a leader's influence within their organization.

7 TAILORED DEVELOPMENT STRATEGIES

- Based on the insights garnered, LP facilitates the creation of personalized development programs that target specific growth areas, ensuring that the leader is equipped to handle the multifaceted demands of their role.

LP can be applied to high-stakes executive recruitment, leadership development programs, team building and organizational restructuring. In the educational domain, it can inform the design of advanced leadership curricula and executive training programs. LP stands at the forefront of innovative leadership assessment and development by adopting a holistic and investigative approach to understanding leaders.

Biofeedback and Coaching Sessions with Horses

Biofeedback instrumentation is incorporated as an auxiliary technique, analogous to the polygraph, in detecting physiological responses. Specifically, sensors track fluctuations in respiration patterns, HRV, electrodermal activity and muscular tension during staged simulations of crises, conflicts and emotionally charged events. This enables trained specialists to evaluate a leader's innate self-regulation capabilities and gain further insights into their cognitive-affective processing under duress that may not be readily apparent from psychological inventories or overt behaviors alone. The resulting biological metrics essentially function as "stress biomarkers" that can be mapped along with the psychometric data to construct a richly layered composite depiction of the qualities and developmental needs that characterize a given leader. In turn, this multimodal profiling approach can be leveraged in the context of high-potential coaching interventions and executive education to strengthen targeted competencies related to composure, decision-making and strategic thinking in high-pressure situations. The biofeedback tracker monitors their physiological state as the leaders engage with the horses. This lets coaches observe how the leaders' interactions with the horses influence their real-time emotional regulation and stress levels. Combining biofeedback tracking with equine-assisted coaching creates a dynamic learning environment where leaders receive immediate feedback on their responses and behaviors.

The efficacy of equine-assisted coaching lies in the thoughtful design of coaching sessions that channel the unique attributes of horses as partners, drawing on scientific research in experiential learning, human-animal interactions and leadership development. Integrating experiential activities, reflective exercises and real-time interactions with horses encourages a deeper connection between participants and the coaching process. By structuring activities that align with specific leadership competencies, participants gain insights into their strengths and areas for development tangibly and memorably. By leveraging biofeedback data, coaches can provide personalized feedback and coaching to reinforce effective behaviors and address areas for improvement. Biofeedback baseline measurements are also conducted over a defined period to capture physiological data, including HRV and respiration patterns. This baseline data is then used to establish a holistic view of the leader's psychometrics and physiological responses. These insights provide valuable information regarding stress management and emotional regulation, allowing coaches to tailor their approach to support the leader's development journey.

STEP 1: SENSOR PLACEMENT

- The client is fitted with an HRV sensor, typically around the write or chest.
- The coach ensures that the client is comfortable with the sensor and the horse, fostering a safe and open environment.

STEP 2: BASELINE MEASUREMENT

- The initial part of the session is dedicated to recording the client's baseline HRV in a calm state, both in and out of the presence of the horse, to gauge the initial response to the equine environment.
- This baseline serves as a reference point for measuring the client's progress throughout the session.

STEP 3: THOUGHTFUL HORSE SELECTION

- Before undertaking any coaching sessions, the coach must set up the client for success by choosing the right horses to work with. Commence by engaging in a discerning process of horse selection. This pivotal step involves carefully curating horses celebrated for their serene and gentle temperaments, ideally possessing prior experience in coaching settings.
- Concomitantly, prioritize the well-being of these equine partners through comprehensive health assessments, ensuring their comfort and readiness for participation in coaching interactions. Clients can also intuitively choose a horse from a team of horses who have been vetted and with whom they feel a deep connection or inspiration. As long as the horse has a foundation of health and a gentle temperament, the horse's specific training in certain areas is not the paramount concern.

STEP 4: PRIORITIZING PHYSICAL SAFETY

- Methodically survey the coaching area to eliminate potential hazards, such as sharp objects or uneven terrain.
- Outfit participants with necessary safety equipment, including helmets, closed-toe and sturdy footwear, gloves to protect hands from blisters and improve grip, and appropriate clothing, such as comfortable long pants that allow for a full range of motion.
- Create a clear emergency plan that includes a mobile phone that is accessible for emergency calls and knowledge of the location of the nearest hospital.
- Require signed consent and waiver forms that fully disclose important information. Participants should be fully informed of the risks of working with animals and sign waivers acknowledging their understanding and acceptance of them before participating.
- Ensure that each session is paired with professional supervision—a professional with experience in equine management and safety should always supervise the sessions.

STEP 5: PROFICIENCY IN EQUINE COMMUNICATION

- Dedicate time to educate participants on primary equine body language before participants start working with the horses' feet to the ground and how their equine partners may react to the participants' voice and body language, unlocking the ability to interpret a horse's emotional state.
- Share with the participants the basic knowledge to recognize crucial indicators such as ear position, tail movement, and stance, all of which provide valuable insights into the horse's intentions and feelings.

STEP 6: CULTIVATING RESPECT AND BOUNDARIES

Emphasize the pivotal role of respect in human-horse interactions and encourage participants to honor the horse's boundaries. Educate participants on recognizing and respecting the horse's personal space, comfort levels and communication signals. Topics that are important to convey to participants include:

- Personal Space: Just like humans, horses have a bubble of personal space that they prefer others not invade. Explain the concept of flight zone, the area surrounding a horse that, when entered, may cause them to move away. Encourage participants to approach a horse slowly, allowing the horse to come to them when it feels comfortable.
- Body Language: Teach participants about the subtleties of horse body language, such as pinned ears, swishing tail or avoidance behavior, which signal discomfort or irritation. Emphasize the importance of backing off and giving the horse more space when these signs are observed.
- Gentle Handling: Horses respond best to calm and gentle handling. Abrupt movements or loud noises can be startling. Instruct participants on how to touch and handle horses in a reassuring and non-threatening way.
- Observation: Encourage participants to spend time simply observing the horse before interacting. This observation helps them learn to read the horse's mood and receptiveness to interaction.
- Positive Reinforcement: Advise participants to use positive reinforcement, such as gentle praise or treats (when appropriate), to build a trusting relationship.

If a participant disrespects a horse's boundaries, it's important to address the situation immediately and assertively, without creating a confrontation:

- Immediate Intervention: Calmly but firmly stop the interaction. It is crucial to ensure the safety of both the horse and the participant.
- Educate: Use the moment as an educational opportunity. Explain what boundary was crossed and why respecting the horse's comfort zone is important.

- Demonstrate: Show the correct way to approach and interact with the horse, modeling respect for its boundaries.
- Reiterate Safety: Remind participants that respecting boundaries is not just about being considerate; it's also about safety. Horses can react unpredictably when they feel threatened or uncomfortable.
- Reflect: Encourage the participant to reflect on the interaction and consider how they might feel if their boundaries were ignored. This can help build empathy and understanding.
- Follow-Up: If necessary, discuss the incident privately and go into detail about respecting boundaries, ensuring it doesn't happen again.
- Moving Forward: Instill qualities of kindness and patience, fostering an atmosphere where horses are regarded as equal partners in the coaching process.

STEP 7: FOSTERING AN EMPATHETIC ATMOSPHERE

Promote participants' confidence when approaching horses, underlining the significance of maintaining calmness and articulating clear intentions. When a participant is nervous about approaching a horse for the first time, it's important to acknowledge their feelings and provide guidance to help them build confidence. Here are steps you might take to support them:

- Acknowledge Their Feelings: Start by acknowledging that it's normal to feel nervous when trying something new, especially when interacting with large animals like horses. Assure them that feeling nervous is okay and support them.
- Educate on Safety: Provide a brief safety overview, explaining how to approach a horse safely, where to stand, and the importance of moving calmly and deliberately.
- Teach About Horse Behavior: Explain some basic horse behavior and body language. Understanding how a horse may react can help the participant feel more in control of the situation.
- Demonstrate First: Show the participant how to approach a horse by demonstrating it. Walk up to the horse confidently yet calmly, stop a few feet away, and allow the horse to acknowledge your presence before moving closer.
- Start with Small Steps: Encourage the participant to start with small steps. They might begin by simply standing near the horse, then gradually moving closer as they feel comfortable.
- Use Breathing Techniques: Teach them a simple breathing exercise to help manage their anxiety. Deep, controlled breaths can help calm both the participant and the horse.
- Encourage Observation: Have them spend some time observing the horse from a distance to get comfortable with its movements and demeanor.

- Offer Support: Stand by their side during the first approach to offer physical and emotional support.
- Positive Reinforcement: Provide positive feedback for any progress made, no matter how small. Encouragement can boost confidence.
- Allow the Client to Retreat if Needed: If they feel overwhelmed, allow them to step back and take a break. Respect their limits.
- Build a Connection: Once they're close enough, guide them on how to offer their hand to the horse to sniff, which is a friendly and non-threatening way to start building a connection.
- Reflect on the Experience: After the interaction, discuss what went well and what could be improved next time. This reflection can reinforce positive aspects and prepare them for future interactions.

Creating an empathetic atmosphere where humans and horses experience a sense of security and recognition is important.

STEP 8: DEFINE CLEAR COACHING OBJECTIVES

Commence by articulating precise coaching objectives closely aligned with desired leadership competencies or the objectives the client wishes to work on. A few coaching objectives that could be beneficial to focus on during such sessions include:

- Developing Emotional Intelligence: Enhancing awareness of one's own emotions and the emotions of others, and learning how to manage and respond to these emotions effectively.
- Improving Non-Verbal Communication: Gaining insight into body language and other non-verbal cues that leaders give off, learning how to read these signals in others, and understanding their impact on team dynamics.
- Building Trust and Rapport: Learning how to establish and maintain trust with team members, including understanding the importance of consistency and authenticity in actions and communication.
- Enhancing Decision-Making Skills: Focusing on making clear, confident and empathetic decisions considering the team's well-being and objectives.
- Cultivating Presence and Mindfulness: Developing the ability to be fully present and engaged, improving focus and reducing the impact of distractions on performance.
- Strengthening Leadership Presence: Projecting confidence and clarity in leadership roles and learning to command respect while remaining approachable.
- Improving Conflict Resolution Skills: Handling conflicts constructively, learning to navigate disagreements and fostering a collaborative environment for problem-solving.

- Fostering Team Collaboration: Encouraging a collaborative spirit within teams, understanding group dynamics and leveraging the strengths of each team member.
- Enhancing Adaptability and Flexibility: Building the capacity to adapt to change, embrace new challenges and respond flexibly to unexpected situations.
- Personal Growth and Self-Reflection: Encouraging introspection about personal strengths and areas for growth, setting personal development goals and aligning personal values with professional conduct. Identify specific skills or behaviors that participants should develop or refine during the coaching process (more in Chapter 3).

STEP 9: SELECTING APPROPRIATE ACTIVITIES

Choose experiential activities that seamlessly align with the client's defined objectives. Activities can range from grooming and leading to unstructured interactions with horses or simply being in proximity to the animal while their HRV is monitored. Clients can also choose the horse they feel most connected to or inspired by, regardless of specific training. In equine-assisted coaching, activities can be categorized into two main types: passive and active, as described by Talia Soldevila Nightingale. Passive activities involve leaders observing the horses and interpreting their behaviors, using these observations to draw parallels to leadership and team dynamics. On the other hand, active activities require direct engagement with the horses, where participants perform tasks involving interacting with, leading or working alongside the horses.

Passive activities include watching how horses interact in the herd, noticing the natural hierarchy and observing communication styles. Leaders can learn from passive observation by seeing how horses establish leadership, set boundaries and communicate needs without words. For instance, a passive activity might involve participants observing a herd from a distance to identify roles within the herd, power dynamics and how horses negotiate space and relationships. These insights can then be discussed and related to workplace dynamics and leadership roles.

Active activities are more hands-on and require participants to enter the arena with the horse. Leaders may engage in activities such as leading a horse through an obstacle course, grooming or other tasks that necessitate clear communication and the establishment of trust. For example, an active activity could involve a participant leading a horse around a set of obstacles, necessitating a leader's clear intent, calmness and non-verbal communication skills. Such interactions provide immediate feedback on the leader's effectiveness and presence.

Both passive and active approaches offer unique benefits. Passive activities can help leaders become more aware of their observation skills and the importance of non-verbal communication. In contrast, active encounters provide a dynamic way to practice leadership skills and receive real-time feedback from the horses. By incorporating both types of activities, a comprehensive equine-assisted coaching program can cater to a wide range of learning styles and objectives, offering participants a rich and varied learning experience.[17] Furthermore, the coach can also instruct the client on how to use breathing techniques and mindfulness to modulate their HRV and, by extension, their emotional state.

STEP 10: FACILITATE STRUCTURED REFLECTION

After each activity, conduct structured reflection sessions to draw out participants' observations, emotions and insights. Structured reflection sessions following equine-assisted activities can be conducted through various methods to deepen the learning experience and solidify the insights gained during the activities. Some effective ways to facilitate these reflection sessions are:

- Group Discussion: Engage participants in a facilitated discussion where they share their observations and emotions. This can be done in a circle, allowing each person to voice their experiences and listen to others, fostering collective learning.
- Journaling: Encourage participants to write about their experiences in a journal or log. Writing can help individuals process their thoughts and emotions more deeply and provide a personal record to look back on.
- One-on-One Debrief: Have individual conversations with participants to discuss their insights. This allows for more private reflection and can help participants open up about their experiences.
- Guided Imagery: Lead a meditation or visualization exercise to help participants recall their experiences with the horse and reflect on the emotions and insights that arose.
- Artistic Expression: Allow participants to draw or create something representing their experience. This can be particularly beneficial for those who express themselves better non-verbally.
- Role-Playing: Have participants re-enact certain moments from the activities to explore different perspectives and outcomes.
- Question Prompts: Provide prompts to guide reflection, such as "What surprised you about your interaction with the horse?" or "What did you learn about yourself as a leader?"
- Feedback Session: Discuss what you observed as a coach and how these observations relate to the participant's behavior and leadership style.
- Action Planning: Help participants create an action plan based on their insights, which they can implement in their leadership role.

By combining these methods, you can cater to different learning styles and preferences, ensuring that all participants can engage in meaningful reflection that will enhance their learning experience and solidify their development as leaders. Encourage participants to delve into their experiences, fostering deeper self-awareness and understanding.

STEP 11: PROMOTE SELF-AWARENESS

Assist them in connecting newfound insights to real-life leadership scenarios, reinforcing the practical applicability of their learnings. Consider incorporating video recordings of activities for participants to review and further enhance their self-awareness. Employ open-ended questions to guide participants in exploring their thoughts and emotions. Open-ended questions are a powerful tool in coaching to facilitate deeper reflection and insight. These questions encourage participants to explore their thoughts and emotions in a non-directive way, allowing for self-discovery and personal growth. Examples of open-ended questions that can be used in reflection sessions following equine-assisted activities include:
   Self-Reflection:

- "What did you notice about your reactions to the horse's behavior?"
- "How did you feel when the horse responded to your actions?"

Leadership Insights:

- "What did this activity reveal to you about your leadership style?"
- "In what ways did the horse act as a mirror for your leadership approach?"

Emotional Intelligence:

- "How did you manage your emotions during the activity?"
- "What did you learn about the connection between your emotions and the horse's reactions?"

Communication:

- "What challenges did you encounter while communicating with the horse?"
- "How might these communication skills translate to your interactions with your team?"

Problem-Solving and Decision Making:

- "What strategies did you use to overcome obstacles during the activity?"
- "How do you see these problem-solving skills applying to challenges in your work?"

Relationship Building:

- "How did you go about establishing a connection with the horse?"
- "What can this experience teach you about building trust with others?"

Adaptability and Flexibility:

- "How did you adapt your approach based on the horse's behavior?"
- "What lessons can you take from this about being flexible in leadership?"

Conflict Resolution:

- "How did you respond to moments of disagreement or resistance from the horse?"
- "What insights can you gain from this about resolving conflicts in your team?"

Personal Growth:

- "What surprised you the most about your interaction with the horse?"
- "How has this experience influenced your perspective on personal growth and development?"

STEP 12: INTEGRATE AND FOLLOW UP

Encourage discussions, particularly in group settings, to facilitate peer learning and to process what happened during the activities. Participants can share their experiences and insights, exploring how these directly relate to their leadership challenges and potential solutions.

Toward the end of each session, the client reflects on their experience and discusses how the insights gained can be applied to their leadership practice. The coach helps the client develop a plan for integrating the biofeedback techniques into their daily routine, such as using breathing exercises before a meeting or employing mindfulness during stressful tasks. Follow-up sessions are scheduled to reinforce the techniques and track long-term progress.

Following these practical steps, you can craft leadership coaching sessions with horses that offer participants tangible insights and foster personal growth. Tailor each session to your unique coaching objectives and group dynamics, ensuring an enriching experience for all involved. Over time, you'll refine your approach and witness the transformative power of equine-assisted coaching firsthand.

Applying Skills in Leadership Scenarios

For sustainable growth, leaders need to bridge insights about personal tendencies gained through equine activities into real-world practice. Facilitated role-plays can simulate workplace situations and provide opportunities to apply relationship skills. Adding horses as participants maintains the experiential immediacy that drives development and self-awareness.

For example, a leader working to improve confidence could be asked to deliver a presentation on a proposed strategy to an executive team, with a horse representing each team member. The unpredictable responses of the horses provide a visceral mirror into how the leader's vocal tones, body language and capacity to think on their feet impact the ability to persuade. Coaches look for signs of stress physiology kicking in, such as increased heart rate or blood pressure revealed by biofeedback sensors. They guide the leader using breathing techniques to maintain embodied poise and quiet internal noise. This embodies confidence as an inner state projected through aligned words and non-verbal presence.

In another scenario, leaders may role-play a tense one-on-one conversation with a direct report who is not meeting expectations. With a horse participant, the dynamic becomes palpable as the horse responds to minute signals of boundaries being conveyed or aggressive energy. Guidance helps the leader practice asserting needs while listening empathetically. Biofeedback monitors stress signals, while observation provides feedback on tones, gestures and responsiveness. This builds skills for delivering constructive feedback with care. Enacting leadership contexts experientially with horses provides opportunities to apply relationship competencies in elevated yet safer conditions.

The persistent feedback and unbiased mirroring of equine responses accelerate the integration of learning into leadership practice. Combining biofeedback and coaching ensures development is embodied for maximal translation from training to real-world settings.

Toward a Holistic Understanding of Leadership

By bringing together the threads of horse-assisted wisdom, psychometric rigor and the objectivity of biofeedback, the coach can present a leadership coaching paradigm that is greater than the sum of its parts. It proposes a holistic model that addresses the leader as a composite of mind, body and behavior, functioning within the intricacies of a complex social and organizational fabric. By reflecting on the future of leadership development, coaches help leaders envision a world where leaders are assessed for their competencies and deeply understood in the full context of their roles and potential for impact.

Notes

1 Roberts, M. (1996). *The man who listens to horses*. Random House.
2 Rauen, J. E. (2017). *The effects of equine assisted learning on emotional intelligence competencies and leadership skills*. Eastern Kentucky University Honors Theses Student Scholarship. https://encompass.eku.edu/honors_theses.
3 Reiner, R. (2008). Integrating a portable biofeedback device into clinical practice for patients with anxiety disorders: Results of a pilot study. *Applied Psychophysiology and Biofeedback*, 33(1), 55–61.
4 Rauen, J. E. (2017). *The effects of equine assisted learning on emotional intelligence competencies and leadership skills*. Eastern Kentucky University Honors Theses Student Scholarship. https://encompass.eku.edu/honors_theses.
5 Mehrabian, A. (2017). *Nonverbal communication*. Routledge.
6 Rauen, J. E. (2017). *The effects of equine assisted learning on emotional intelligence competencies and leadership skills*. Eastern Kentucky University Honors Theses Student Scholarship. https://encompass.eku.edu/honors_theses.
7 Roberts, M. (1996). *The man who listens to horses*. Random House.
8 Gehrke, E. K., Baldwin, A., & Schiltz, P. M. (2021). Heart rate variability in horses during equine-assisted activities. *Journal of Equine Veterinary Science*, 100, 103265.
9 Rauen, J. E. (2017). *The effects of equine assisted learning on emotional intelligence competencies and leadership skills*. Eastern Kentucky University Honors Theses Student Scholarship. https://encompass.eku.edu/honors_theses/490/.
10 Roberts, M. (1996). *The man who listens to horses*. Random House.
11 Krishnamurti, J. (1956). *Education and the significance of life*. Harper & Row.
12 Laborde, S., Mosley, E., & Thayer, J. F. (2017). Heart rate variability and cardiac vagal tone in psychophysiological research: Recommendations for experiment planning, data analysis, and data reporting. *Frontiers in Psychology*, 8, 213.
13 David, S. (2016). *Emotional agility: Get unstuck, embrace change, and thrive in work and life*. Penguin.
14 McCraty, R., & Zayas, M. A. (2014). Cardiac coherence, self-regulation, autonomic stability, and psychosocial well-being. *Frontiers in Psychology*, 5, 1090.
15 Laborde, S., Mosley, E., & Thayer, J. F. (2017). Heart rate variability and cardiac vagal tone in psychophysiological research: Recommendations for experiment planning, data analysis, and data reporting. *Frontiers in Psychology*, 8, 213.
16 Hassett, A. L., Radvanski, D. C., Vaschillo, E. G., Vaschillo, B., Sigal, L. H., Karavidas, M. K., ... & Lehrer, P. M. (2007). A pilot study of the efficacy of heart rate variability (HRV) biofeedback in patients with fibromyalgia. *Applied Psychophysiology and Biofeedback*, 32(1), 1.
17 Nightingale, S. T. (2010). *El Maestro equino: coaching, psicoterapia y aprendizaje asistido con equinos*. El mundo de las terapias.

Chapter 5

Embracing Continuous Growth

A Lifelong Leadership Journey

The transformative journey through leadership coaching with horses, bio-feedback and psychometrics is a profound experience that transcends the boundaries of traditional leadership development. It signifies the dawn of a sustained practice where leaders continually evolve, not just as professionals, but as individuals navigating the complexities of life's ever-changing land-scapes. This ongoing journey is characterized by integrating self-awareness, emotional agility and physiological insights into daily leadership practices, fostering a culture of perpetual personal and professional evolution where growth becomes a goal and a way of life. At the heart of this innovative coaching methodology lies the synergistic integration of three powerful ele-ments: the wisdom of horses, the insights of biofeedback technology and the depth of psychometric assessments. Each component contributes uniquely to the overall effectiveness of the approach, creating a holistic and transformative experience for leaders.

The Unique Benefits and Integration of Equine-Assisted Coaching with Modern Science

In concluding our exploration of modern leadership development tools, we revisit the integral roles played by horses, biofeedback technology and psy-chometric assessments, each offering unique insights into the art and science of leadership.

Horses, with their keen sensitivity and inherently non-predatory nature, serve as profound catalysts in the development of emotional intelligence and authentic leadership. Through equine-assisted coaching, leaders are offered a mirror reflecting their emotional and behavioral states, facilitating a deep dive into personal growth. This form of experiential learning promotes enhanced self-awareness and improved communication skills. The impact of such interactions can be transformative, as demonstrated by leaders like the CEO who, through groundwork exercises with horses, learned the value of empathy and adjusted their leadership approach to be more attuned to the needs and feelings of others.

DOI: 10.4324/9781032683843-6

Biofeedback technology further enriches this learning landscape by providing empirical data that bridges the gap between internal experiences and observable outcomes. This technology measures physiological responses such as heart rate variability and muscle tension, allowing leaders to see in real-time how their emotional states influence their physical bodies. Such insights are invaluable for mastering stress management and emotional regulation, critical skills for any high-performing leader. The journey of a senior executive who utilized biofeedback to uncover and mitigate the impacts of chronic stress exemplifies how such tools can lead to significant professional and personal enhancements.

Meanwhile, psychometric assessments offer a comprehensive overview of an individual's personality traits, cognitive abilities and behavioral tendencies, which, when integrated with insights gained from equine-assisted coaching and biofeedback, create a powerful platform for targeted personal development. Leaders can leverage these detailed analyses to fine-tune their development plans, addressing specific areas such as assertiveness and delegation. This was clearly seen in the case of a leader who, recognizing their weaknesses in these areas through their psychometric profile, embarked on a focused strategy to enhance their leadership capabilities.

Bringing these elements together, the synergy between the intuitive feedback from equine coaching, the objective data provided by biofeedback and the in-depth analysis enabled by psychometric assessments forms a comprehensive model for leadership development. This multifaceted approach does not merely address leadership as a set of skills to be improved but as a complex interaction of emotional, physiological and cognitive components that must be harmonized.

As we look toward the future of leadership development, it becomes increasingly clear that the integration of these diverse methods will be pivotal in shaping leaders who are not only effective in their roles but also genuine, self-aware and profoundly connected to the people they lead. The journey to becoming such a leader is dynamic and continuous, requiring a commitment to exploring these depths and continuously adapting to new insights—a life-long endeavor that promises substantial rewards for those who pursue it with openness and dedication.

Navigating Challenges and Overcoming Obstacles

While the path of leadership development through equine-assisted coaching, biofeedback and psychometric assessments holds immense potential, leaders may face a variety of challenges and obstacles along the way. One of the most common hurdles is resistance to change, as deeply ingrained habits and beliefs can be stubbornly resistant to modification. This resistance is often compounded by the tendency to revert to old behavior patterns or the difficulty in maintaining accountability, which can significantly hinder progress.

To navigate these challenges, it is crucial for leaders to cultivate a mindset of continuous learning and self-reflection. Engaging in regular self-assessment and honest introspection plays a pivotal role in identifying potential roadblocks, thus enabling timely adjustments and course corrections. Such reflective practices help leaders remain flexible and responsive to their evolving understanding of leadership dynamics. Additionally, establishing a supportive network comprising peers, mentors and coaches who appreciate the profound nature of this transformative journey can offer invaluable guidance, encouragement and accountability. This community not only acts as a sounding board but also as a motivational force that pushes leaders to persist in their developmental efforts.

Furthermore, embracing the philosophical foundations of ethical leadership can serve as a powerful catalyst for sustained growth and development. By anchoring their leadership practices in a moral compass, leaders can navigate through temporary challenges and setbacks with greater resilience. Aligning actions with timeless virtues such as integrity, transparency and social responsibility not only enhances personal leadership qualities but also elevates the collective ethos of the organizations they lead. Such principles foster a leadership style that is not only effective but also honorable and admired.

Coaches should encourage leaders to pause and reflect on their leadership journey. What challenges or obstacles did they encounter along the way? How did the principles and practices discussed help them navigate challenges more effectively? Have the leaders write down their thoughts and insights, as the act of reflection itself can deepen their understanding and commitment to personal growth.

By embedding these practices into their development, leaders can ensure that their growth is not only progressive but also introspective and aligned with higher leadership ideals. Such a holistic approach to leadership development not only fosters individual excellence but also cultivates a culture of ethical leadership within organizations, driving them towards greater success and societal contribution. Through continuous learning, ethical grounding, and reflective practice, leaders are equipped to transform challenges into stepping stones for leadership mastery and personal fulfillment.

Integrating Ethical Leadership Principles

As we have seen in the previous chapters, effective leadership transcends the realms of strategic decision-making and skilled communication. It is fundamentally rooted in a deeply ingrained moral code that dictates every action and decision, guiding leaders not just to achieve, but to inspire and transform. This foundational ethical stance underpins the entire structure of leadership, providing a compass that directs leaders toward actions that are not only effective but also righteous and principled. By embracing a strong philosophical foundation for ethical leadership, leaders cultivate a sense of purpose and integrity that echoes far beyond their immediate goals or organizational objectives, reaching into the broader societal impacts of their decisions and actions.

One profound ethical framework that leaders can adopt is the principle of virtue ethics. This approach emphasizes the cultivation of moral character traits such as courage, temperance, justice and wisdom—virtues that Aristotle and other ancient philosophers deemed essential for leading a fulfilled and ethical life. By integrating these virtues into their daily actions and decisions, leaders foster a culture of trust, respect and accountability within their organizations. For instance, courage allows leaders to make difficult decisions in the face of adversity, while justice ensures that fairness prevails in all business dealings and employee interactions. Temperance helps maintain a balanced approach to risk, and wisdom guides the leader to make decisions that consider long-term impacts over short-term gains.

Another powerful ethical principle is that of servant leadership, which shifts the focus from the leader's personal gain to the growth and well-being of the team members. This approach prioritizes the needs and development of others, creating a leadership style that is inherently altruistic and generous. Servant leadership empowers individuals, fostering an organizational culture where every team member feels valued and motivated to contribute their best. This kind of environment is highly conducive to collaboration, innovation and collective success, as it nurtures a shared purpose and deep commitment among all team members. When leaders operate from a standpoint of service, they inspire loyalty and drive that can lead to extraordinary outcomes.

These ethical leadership traits—virtue ethics and servant leadership—are vividly demonstrated and reinforced in equine-assisted learning environments. Working with horses provides a unique opportunity for leaders to experience and embody these principles firsthand. Horses, as sensitive and responsive beings, react not only to the explicit commands they are given but also to the intentions and emotions behind those commands. This interaction requires leaders to practice congruence between their internal states and external actions. For instance, a horse may become anxious or hesitant if the leader's outward confidence does not match their internal fear or uncertainty, mirroring back the incongruence that can often occur in human interactions.

Through equine-assisted learning, leaders can better understand the importance of authenticity and integrity in their leadership style. They learn that just as a horse requires a leader to be genuine and consistent, so too do human teams require their leaders to be trustworthy and ethical. This form of learning also emphasizes the power of non-verbal communication and the importance of emotional intelligence—skills that are crucial for effective leadership but often overlooked in traditional business environments.

By adopting these ethical frameworks and engaging in experiential learning with horses, leaders can significantly enhance their understanding and application of ethical principles in their professional and personal lives. They can transform their approach to leadership, grounding it not only in achieving objectives and milestones but also in fostering an ethical, supportive and empowering environment for all stakeholders. This holistic approach to leadership not only improves organizational performance but also contributes positively to the community and society at large, setting a standard for ethical conduct and responsible leadership that resonates well beyond the confines of the boardroom.

Have the leader consider their personal values and ethical principles, asking how they align with the concepts of virtue ethics and servant leadership. Identify specific actions or behaviors they could adopt to integrate these principles into their leadership practice better. Have them reflect on how embracing ethical leadership could positively impact their organization and those they lead.

Embracing Philosophical Foundations for Ethical Leadership

This journey of leadership development presents a unique opportunity for leaders to introspectively examine and refine their moral compass. It allows them to align themselves with universal truths and ethical principles that go beyond personal desires and motivations, fostering a leadership style that is both principled and impactful.

Furthermore, this deep commitment to ethical leadership can serve as a guiding light in times of uncertainty and complexity. When faced with challenging decisions or ethical dilemmas, a well-defined moral code provides a clear path forward, ensuring that choices are not only effective but also just and fair. This approach builds trust and integrity within the team and organization, creating a strong foundation that can weather both internal challenges and external pressures.

Diagnose: Unveiling the Moral Code

The initial phase of cultivating ethical leadership begins with a profound introspection into one's own moral framework. This step is crucial, as it involves diagnosing and understanding the underlying principles that guide a leader's decisions and actions. Leaders must discern between cause and matter, delving deeply into the philosophical underpinnings that define their worldview and decision-making processes. Recognizing the ephemeral nature of existence while embracing the eternal truths that lie beyond our immediate understanding is fundamental in this journey.

This realization of life's transient nature can profoundly impact a leader's perspective, encouraging the development of humility and acceptance. These virtues are essential as they allow leaders to see beyond the superficial aspects of day-to-day challenges and focus on longer-term, more significant impacts. With this mindset, leaders are better equipped to make decisions that are not only effective in the immediate context but are also aligned with enduring ethical standards.

Moreover, this understanding fosters a grounding in universal principles, steering leaders away from decisions driven by fleeting desires or momentary gains. It encourages a shift towards actions that promote lasting good, reinforcing the importance of ethical integrity in leadership roles. This perspective is critical in today's fast-paced, often volatile business environments where short-term gains can be enticing. By maintaining a focus on long-term ethical considerations, leaders can avoid the pitfalls of opportunistic strategies and instead foster practices that ensure sustainable success.

Cultivating this deep moral understanding also enables leaders to inspire and influence their teams and organizations positively. When leaders operate from a place of ethical clarity and conviction, they set a powerful example for others within the organization, promoting a culture of integrity and ethical behavior. This influence helps to instill a shared commitment to ethical standards throughout the organization, enhancing collective moral judgment and reinforcing a positive organizational ethos.

Ultimately, the process of unveiling and understanding one's moral code is not a one-time activity but a continuous endeavor that requires ongoing reflection and reassessment. As leaders grow and encounter new challenges, their understanding of ethics might evolve, necessitating regular re-evaluation to ensure their actions remain consistent with their core ethical beliefs. This dynamic process of ethical introspection and application helps leaders not only to navigate their path with moral clarity but also to lead by example, fostering an environment where ethical considerations are at the forefront of decision-making processes.

Thus, diagnosing and continually refining the moral code is essential for any leader committed to ethical excellence and transformative leadership. It is the cornerstone upon which the edifice of sustainable leadership is built, ensuring that the pursuit of success is always aligned with the highest standards of ethical conduct.

Drawing inspiration from Nietzsche's profound insights, leaders understand that human nature finds its fulfillment in contemplation—a form of intuition that guides one towards good and right conduct in practical life.

Prescribe: Philosophical Exercises for Auto-Discipline

With a deeper understanding of their own moral framework, leaders are well-positioned to prescribe philosophical exercises that cultivate auto-discipline and moral fortitude. These exercises are not merely routine tasks but are profound practices rooted in ancient wisdom and timeless philosophies that have guided countless leaders across centuries. Through these philosophical disciplines, leaders can develop core virtues such as fortitude, sincerity and loyalty. These virtues are essential for building a robust character that consistently upholds integrity and demonstrates resilience in the face of adversity.

One effective approach is for leaders to regularly engage with philosophical texts and teachings that emphasize the development of inner strength and ethical leadership. By studying these works, leaders can draw inspiration and practical guidance on living and leading ethically. Additionally, incorporating practices such as meditation, reflective journaling and structured ethical debates within their routine can help leaders internalize these virtues. Meditation allows for deep self-reflection and the cultivation of peace and stability within the mind, which is crucial for sound decision-making. Reflective journaling can serve as a means to solidify learnings and commitments to ethical practices, while structured debates provide a platform to explore and strengthen one's arguments and principles under scrutiny.

By nurturing the internal order of body, soul and intelligence, leaders can create a balanced and harmonious internal environment. This holistic development is vital for leaders as it fosters a comprehensive understanding and alignment of their thoughts, emotions and actions. When leaders have this internal order well-established, they are better equipped to retreat within themselves to renew their principles and realign their actions whenever discrepancies arise. This practice ensures that their leadership is not only effective but also morally grounded and consistent over time.

Moreover, these philosophical exercises encourage leaders to foster a mindset of integrity that transcends the personal and touches the universal. This broadened perspective enables leaders to not just navigate their own moral dilemmas but also to inspire and lead others in ethical decision-making. By setting an example of moral leadership, they cultivate an organizational culture where integrity, sincerity and loyalty are not just expected but are lived values.

In the dynamic and often challenging landscape of leadership, the ability to remain steadfast in one's ethical convictions while adapting to changing circumstances is invaluable. The prescribed philosophical exercises are tools that build such capability, ensuring that leaders do not merely react to external pressures but respond thoughtfully and consistently in alignment with their deep-seated ethical beliefs.

Therefore, prescribing philosophical exercises for auto-discipline isn't just about personal growth; it's about fostering a sustainable model of leadership that thrives on moral fortitude and integrity. This proactive approach to ethical cultivation not only prepares leaders to handle present challenges but also equips them to face future uncertainties with a grounded sense of purpose and a clear moral compass.

Verify: Applying Principles in Practice

As leaders advance on their path of self-discovery and ethical maturation, it becomes imperative for them to verify and affirm their principles through consistent action. Leading by virtue requires more than just professing ethical ideals; it demands the integration and embodiment of these principles in every facet of one's professional and personal life. This practice of verification ensures that the values leaders champion are not only spoken but are vividly demonstrated in their actions.

For leaders, this means maintaining an unwavering commitment to virtues like justice, honesty and the common good, regardless of the circumstances they face. Whether navigating the highs of success or enduring times of hardship, ethical leaders are tasked with the challenge of consistently aligning their actions with their moral beliefs. This steadfast adherence is crucial, not only in keeping their integrity intact but also in serving as a model for others within their influence.

To effectively verify these principles in practice, leaders can implement regular self-assessments and solicit feedback from trusted colleagues and mentors. These assessments should focus on how well their decisions align with their ethical standards, particularly during critical decision-making moments. Leaders should ask themselves and others if their actions in both public and private spheres demonstrate the virtues they advocate for.

Additionally, implementing transparent decision-making processes that invite scrutiny and encourage accountability can help leaders maintain their ethical commitments. Such processes ensure that decisions are not made in isolation but are subject to the diverse perspectives and insights of a broader group, which can help uphold the principles of fairness and collective benefit.

Moreover, leaders should actively seek opportunities to apply their ethical principles in ways that contribute positively to their communities and society at large. This could mean engaging in corporate social responsibility initiatives, supporting ethical practices in their industry, or advocating for policies that promote equity and justice. By doing so, leaders not only verify their commitment to their values but also contribute to the social fabric, enhancing the well-being of others beyond the confines of their organization.

The practice of verifying ethical principles in action also involves reflecting on and learning from instances where there might have been a shortfall. Understanding these moments provides invaluable insights that can fortify a leader's moral resolve and inform future decisions, ensuring they are better prepared to act ethically under varying circumstances.

Encouraging: Equality and Unity

In today's world, the role of true leadership is crucial in bridging gaps between varying identities and ideologies. Such leadership transcends the usual boundaries set by society, fostering a profound sense of unity and equality among all individuals. By acknowledging and valuing every person's inherent dignity and worth, leaders have the opportunity to forge inclusive environments that not only celebrate diversity but also promote inclusivity.

This approach to leadership goes beyond merely tolerating differences; it involves actively engaging with varied perspectives to enrich organizational culture and operational effectiveness. Leaders who embrace this model serve as catalysts for positive change, encouraging their organizations to look past conventional social constructs and appreciate the interconnectedness that binds all people together. This shift toward a more inclusive perspective is essential for creating spaces where everyone feels valued and empowered to contribute their best.

To effectively encourage equality and unity, leaders must implement policies and practices that ensure equal opportunities for all, regardless of background, identity or belief. Furthermore, leaders should actively work to dismantle any existing barriers to inclusion within their organizations, be they cultural, structural or procedural.

Leaders can also foster unity by facilitating open and respectful dialogues about diversity and inclusion. These discussions can help raise awareness about the different challenges individuals face and explore ways the organization can address them. By encouraging a culture of listening and learning, leaders can help everyone in the organization understand and appreciate the unique contributions of each member, which strengthens team cohesion and enhances collective problem-solving capabilities.

Moreover, leaders should lead by example, demonstrating commitment to these values in their everyday actions and decisions. This visible commitment helps to cement the importance of unity and equality within the organizational culture, making it clear that these values are not just rhetorical but are central to the organization's identity and mission.

Encouraging equality and unity is not a one-time effort but a continuous process that requires constant attention and dedication. It involves a commitment to personal growth and organizational development that adapts to changing demographics and societal norms. By steadfastly upholding these principles, leaders not only enhance the moral fiber of their organizations but also contribute to a more just and equitable society.

After all, leaders who champion these principles of equality and unity not only inspire their teams but also drive their organizations towards greater innovation and success. In doing so, they prove that diversity is not a barrier to be overcome but a rich resource to be embraced, offering varied insights and perspectives that can lead to more effective and creative solutions to the challenges facing modern organizations.

Confirm: Leadership as a Way of Being

Leadership transcends the mere acts associated with guiding others—it embodies a comprehensive way of being. It reflects deeply ingrained values, principles and the very character of the individual. In today's performance-oriented society, where self-esteem is often tied to external recognition and achievements, true leadership emerges not from the accolades or milestones achieved, but from an unwavering commitment to ethical action and steadfast moral integrity.

True leadership is defined by the consistent application of one's core values across all aspects of life and work, regardless of the challenges or temptations to deviate from these principles. It involves more than just making decisions or issuing commands; it's about setting a moral standard that others aspire to emulate. Leaders who genuinely embody their values demonstrate through their actions that success is not merely about results but about the journey and the means by which those results are achieved.

By incorporating timeless virtues such as wisdom, compassion and humility into their daily conduct, leaders do more than achieve goals—they inspire greatness in others. Wisdom allows leaders to see beyond the immediate, to understand deeper truths and apply them. Compassion engenders a leadership style that values and respects all contributors, fostering an environment where everyone feels valued and understood. Humility keeps leaders grounded, reminding them that no matter the heights they reach, they are still part of a larger community with a role to play.

Such leaders encourage others not merely to follow but to embark on their own journeys of moral and ethical growth. This ripple effect can transform organizations and communities, creating a culture where ethical leadership is the norm, not the exception. In doing so, they usher in a new era of leadership—one that's rooted in the eternal truths of humanity and dedicated to the betterment of society at large.

Leadership, then, is a manifestation of one's inner self in outward action. It is about living one's truth and, in doing so, leading others by example. This approach to leadership not only elevates the individual leader but elevates those around them, creating a legacy of integrity and ethical standards that transcends generations. In an age where leadership is often scrutinized, those who lead with a clear moral compass and a commitment to genuine virtues stand out as beacons of hope and pillars of strength.

In embracing leadership as a way of being, leaders forge a path that goes beyond conventional success metrics and towards a definition of success that is rich in integrity and significance. It is through this lens that true leaders are recognized—not just for what they achieve, but for who they are, and how they inspire others to become versions of their best selves. Thus, leadership becomes not just a role to be played, but a life to be lived.

Envisioning the Future of Equine-Assisted Leadership Development

As equine-assisted leadership coaching evolves, embracing future trends and innovations will be crucial to maintaining relevance and effectiveness in a rapidly changing world. Advancements such as virtual reality (VR) simulations, wearable technology and collaborative learning environments hold immense potential for enhancing coaching experiences and driving continued growth and development.

VR Simulations: Immersive VR experiences can create realistic scenarios that mimic the challenges and dynamics of equine-assisted coaching sessions. By integrating biofeedback data and psychometric insights, VR simulations can provide a safe and controlled environment for leaders to practice and refine their skills, allowing for experimentation and iteration without physical limitations.

Wearable Technology: Wearable devices equipped with advanced biometric sensors can offer real-time physiological data collection, enabling leaders to monitor their stress levels, emotional states and overall well-being during coaching sessions and beyond. By integrating this data with psychometric profiles and equine interactions, leaders can gain deeper insights into their reactions and develop personalized self-regulation and emotional resilience strategies.

Collaborative Learning Environments: The future of leadership development may involve the creation of collaborative learning environments, where leaders from diverse backgrounds can come together to share their experiences, exchange insights, and support one another's growth. Through online platforms, virtual coaching sessions, and interactive forums, leaders can engage in collective learning, creating a sense of community and accountability while benefiting from the collective wisdom of their peers.

To support leaders on their continuous development journey, resources such as the Nature Motivation blog (www.nature-motivation.com/blog) and e-learning platforms (www.nature-motivation.com/elearning) offer ongoing guidance, insights and opportunities for advanced training or mentorship. By adapting and integrating emerging technologies, equine-assisted leadership coaching can remain at the forefront of leadership development, unlocking the full potential of leaders for generations to come and paving the way for a future where leadership is not just about achieving results, but about empowering individuals to reach their highest potential and create lasting impacts in the world. Through this holistic and transformative approach, the convergence of equine wisdom, technological insight and psychological depth forms a comprehensive framework for leadership development that transcends traditional coaching methodologies.

Appendix I: List of Exercises

Active Exercises

Introduction to Active Exercises

Active exercises in leadership coaching with horses serve as dynamic tools to enhance real-world skills in a controlled, experiential setting. These activities are designed to simulate challenges that leaders often face in their professional environments. By engaging physically and emotionally with tasks, participants can uncover new insights about their leadership style, problem-solving abilities and interpersonal dynamics.

Active exercises, particularly those involving horses in the context of leadership coaching, capitalize on the immediate feedback provided by these sensitive and responsive animals. Horses react in real-time to human behavior, offering honest and often unfiltered feedback. This can lead to profound revelations about a leader's communication style, emotional intelligence and overall effectiveness in a leadership role.

Development of Core Leadership Skills Through Active Exercises

1   **Communication:** Active exercises that involve horses require clear and intentional communication. Horses, being highly sensitive to non-verbal cues, mirror back the clarity and confidence (or lack thereof) of the leader's cues. This environment pushes leaders to refine their ability to convey clear instructions and feedback, which is crucial in any organizational setting.
2   **Decision-Making:** These exercises place leaders in scenarios where decisions must be made swiftly and effectively with immediate consequences. For instance, navigating a horse through a complex obstacle course requires quick thinking and firm decision-making. This practice develops a leader's ability to assess situations quickly and act decisively, a vital skill in fast-paced business environments.
3   **Adaptability:** Working with horses in varying exercises teaches adaptability—the capability to adjust strategies based on the feedback received from the horse's reactions. Leaders learn to be flexible in their approaches and responsive to the needs and behaviors of others, paralleling the dynamic nature of managing teams or handling client relationships.

Safety Considerations When Working Actively with Horses

Safety is paramount in equine-assisted activities, both for the human participants and the animals involved. Here are several key safety considerations:

1 **Proper Introduction:** Before engaging in active exercises, participants should be properly introduced to the horses, including understanding the basics of horse behavior and how to approach, lead and interact with a horse safely.
2 **Professional Supervision:** All sessions should be overseen by professionals trained in both equine behavior and leadership coaching. This ensures that activities are conducted safely and that both the horses and participants are handled with care.
3 **Appropriate Gear:** Participants should wear appropriate attire, including closed-toe shoes, helmets (if required) and other protective gear to prevent injuries.
4 **Understanding Limits:** It's crucial to understand and respect the physical and emotional limits of both the horses and the participants. Activities should be tailored to suit the experience level of the group and not push the horses or humans beyond what they can handle comfortably.
5 **Emergency Procedures:** Clear procedures should be in place for dealing with emergencies. Participants should be briefed on these procedures, and all necessary first aid equipment should be readily available.

Incorporating these considerations into leadership coaching with horses ensures a safe, respectful and beneficial experience for everyone involved. By focusing on communication, decision-making and adaptability, leaders can develop these essential skills in a unique, impactful way through active exercises with horses.

Exercise 1: Leadership in Motion

- **Objective:** Enhance decision-making skills and assertiveness.
- **Activity Description:**
  - Participant(s) are tasked with leading a horse through a preset course consisting of various obstacles.
  - The course layout should require participants to make decisions rapidly about the path and handling techniques.
- **Tools Needed:** Obstacles such as cones, poles, gates and tarps.
- **Procedure:**
  - Warm-up: Get to know the horse, understand its temperaments and establish initial communication.
  - Walk the course without the horse to plan the route and anticipate challenges.
  - Lead the horse through the course, focusing on clear and assertive communication and body language.

- **Reflection Points:**

  - Discuss how different approaches affected the horse's behavior and course completion.
  - Reflect on personal decision-making styles and how they translate into leadership roles.

Exercise 2: Boundary Setting

- **Objective:** Develop effective communication and boundary-setting skills.
- **Activity Description:** Participant(s) will direct a horse to stay out of a defined area using non-verbal communication techniques.
- **Tools Needed:** Rope or markers to define boundaries.
- **Procedure:**

  - Participants first observe the horse's natural behavior and boundaries.
  - They then use body language to communicate and enforce a boundary without physical contact.

- **Reflection Points:**

  - Evaluate the clarity and effectiveness of non-verbal cues used.
  - Discuss the importance of setting and respecting boundaries in professional environments.

Exercise 3: Pathfinding

- **Objective:** Improve strategic thinking and the ability to anticipate future needs.
- **Activity Description:** Participant(s) create and navigate a complex route that will challenge both them and the horse, involving various tasks that must be completed along the way.
- **Tools Needed:** Various objects to create tasks and obstacles (e.g., balls, flags, buckets).
- **Procedure:**

  - Map out a strategic course that includes tasks that mimic workplace challenges.
  - Lead the horse through the course, adjusting strategies as needed based on the horse's reactions.

- **Reflection Points:**

  - Analyze the planning process and adjustments made during the activity.
  - Discuss how foresight and adaptability are critical in leadership.

Exercise 4: Mirror Leading

- **Objective:** Cultivate empathetic leadership and non-verbal communication skills.
- **Activity Description:** Leaders take turns guiding a horse by mirroring its movements, emphasizing non-verbal cues and emotional attunement.
- **Tools Needed:** A calm, secure area for free movement.
- **Procedure:**

  - Observation: Leaders watch the horse's behavior and movements to understand its pace and mood.
  - Mirroring Action: Without leads or restraints, leaders attempt to synchronize their movements with the horse, fostering a mutual rhythm.
  - Feedback Loop: Participants receive feedback from observers on the harmony and leadership presence displayed.

- **Reflection Points:**

  - How effective were the leaders in adapting their approach to the horse's responses?
  - Discuss the impact of non-verbal leadership cues on team morale and follower engagement.

Exercise 5: Pressure and Release with Blindfolded Leadership

- **Objective:** Master the balance of influence and autonomy while enhancing trust and communication within the team.
- **Activity Description:** The leader is blindfolded and must guide the horse through a series of tasks based solely on verbal cues from team members.
- **Tools Needed:** Blindfold, halter, lead rope and target points (such as cones).
- **Procedure:**

  - Team Briefing: Explain the concepts of pressure and release, and how these can guide the horse with minimal force.
  - Blindfolded Leadership: The blindfolded leader uses the verbal guidance of their team to navigate the horse to various targets, applying gentle pressure on the lead and releasing as the horse complies.
  - Team Coordination: Team members must provide clear, concise instructions to help the leader and horse succeed.

- **Reflection Points:**

  - Reflect on the communication effectiveness and trust dynamics within the team.
  - Discuss the parallels between the exercise and leading teams in a corporate environment where trust and clear directives are crucial.

Passive Exercises

Passive exercises with horses in leadership coaching provide a unique opportunity for introspection, empathy development and emotional management. Unlike active exercises that involve direct interaction and immediate decision-making, passive exercises focus on observation, reflection and the subtle nuances of non-verbal communication. These exercises are designed to deepen leaders' understanding of themselves and others without the need for direct control or action.

Enhancing Introspection, Empathy and Emotional Management

1   **Introspection:** Passive exercises allow participants to observe the natural behaviors of horses from a distance, reflecting on their own internal responses to what they see. For example, watching how a horse reacts to new stimuli or interacts with other horses can mirror back participants' feelings about change or teamwork. This reflection can lead to a deeper understanding of personal biases, fears and motivations.
2   **Empathy:** By observing horses, participants learn to read and interpret non-verbal cues such as body language and facial expressions. Horses communicate primarily through non-verbal signals, and learning to understand these can improve a leader's ability to empathize with others. This skill is transferable to human interactions, enhancing interpersonal relationships and team dynamics.
3   **Emotional Management:** Horses respond directly to the emotional state of those around them. Observing these reactions helps participants recognize the impact of their own emotions on others. This awareness fosters better self-regulation and emotional control, crucial for leaders in managing stress, conflict and motivation within teams.

The Importance of Observing and Reflecting

Passive exercises emphasize the value of observation and reflection over direct interaction. This approach provides several benefits:

• Reduced Bias in Interaction: By removing the direct interaction, participants can observe behaviors and dynamics without the influence of their actions. This can lead to more objective insights into group dynamics and individual behaviors.
• Increased Awareness: Passive observation forces participants to slow down and notice the details they might miss in more active settings. This heightened awareness can lead to improved mindfulness and presence, which are essential for effective leadership.

- Space for Reflection: Without the pressure to react or engage directly, participants have more mental space to process their observations and reflect on their implications. This can lead to more profound personal insights and a clearer understanding of how to apply these learnings in their leadership practices.

Incorporating passive exercises into leadership coaching with horses provides a complementary approach to the more common active techniques. By observing and reflecting, leaders can develop a richer, more nuanced understanding of leadership, communication and emotional intelligence. This holistic approach not only enhances personal growth but also equips leaders with the skills necessary to foster a more empathetic and effective leadership style.

Exercise 1: Observational Learning

- **Objective:** Enhance leaders' emotional intelligence by understanding non-verbal communication.
- **Activity Description:** Participants observe interactions between multiple horses at rest or play.
- **Procedure:**
    - Spend time observing the horses without interacting, noting their body language and interactions.
    - Participants then share their observations and discuss what emotions and behaviors they believe they saw.
- **Reflection Points:**
    - What can human leaders learn from these equine interactions?
    - How does understanding non-verbal cues play a role in leadership effectiveness?

Exercise 2: Mindful Presence

- **Objective:** Cultivate presence, mindfulness and the ability to stay grounded.
- **Activity Description:** Participants engage in a mindfulness session in the presence of horses.
- **Procedure:**
    - Guided mindfulness practices are conducted while in close proximity to the horses, focusing on breathing and the surrounding environment.
    - The calming presence of the horses enhances the mindfulness experience.

- **Reflection Points:**
    - Discuss the impact of the environment and external calmness on internal states.
    - Explore how mindfulness can affect leadership presence and decision-making.

Exercise 3: Silent Communication

- **Objective**: Develop an understanding of the power of silent leadership and non-verbal cues.
- **Activity Description:** Participants attempt to communicate with a horse using only non-verbal cues to direct its movements.
- **Procedure:**
    - Silent Interaction: Without speaking, participants use body language and presence to try to guide the horse's movements.
    - Feedback: Observers provide feedback on the effectiveness of the non-verbal communication strategies used.
- **Reflection Points:**
    - Evaluate which non-verbal techniques were most effective and why.
    - Discuss how these techniques can be translated into leadership practices, particularly in managing teams without overt commands.

Exercise 4: Reflective Observation

- **Objective:** Promote deep reflection on leadership styles and their impacts.
- **Activity Description:** Participants watch a professional handler work with a horse and reflect on the handler's leadership style.
- **Procedure:**
    - Professional Demonstration: A skilled handler demonstrates various techniques to manage and lead a horse.
    - Group Reflection: Participants discuss what they observed, focusing on the handler's approach and the horse's responses.
- **Reflection Points:**
    - Discuss how different leadership styles can lead to different outcomes.
    - Reflect on how adaptability and flexibility in leadership can improve team performance and morale.

Exercise 5: Group Dynamics Analysis

- **Objective:** Analyze group dynamics and leadership roles without direct involvement.

- **Activity Description:** Participants observe a group of horses and identify natural leaders and followers within the group.
- **Procedure:**
  - Group Observation: Watch how a group of horses organizes itself, noting leadership roles and group dynamics.
  - Role Identification: Identify which horses take on leadership roles and which follow, and how they interact.

- **Reflection Points:**
  - Discuss the characteristics that distinguish the leaders from the followers.
  - Reflect on how these dynamics are similar to human team dynamics and what can be learned about effective leadership and team participation.

Developing Your Own Exercises

Creating custom exercises in leadership coaching with horses offers coaches the flexibility to tailor sessions that specifically address the unique leadership development goals of their clients. Personalized sessions can focus on particular areas of need, such as enhancing communication, building trust or improving decision-making skills, ensuring that the exercises are directly relevant and immediately beneficial to participants.

Guidelines for Creating Personalized Leadership Coaching with Horses (LCH)

1   **Assess Needs:** Begin by conducting a thorough assessment of the leadership strengths and weaknesses of the individual, group or team. This step involves different strategies depending on the unit of focus:

   - **Individuals:** Utilize personal interviews, self-assessments and perhaps past performance reviews to identify specific personal development areas.
   - **Groups:** When working with groups, assessments might include group dynamics analysis and observing interactions to identify common patterns or challenges that need addressing.
   - **Teams:** For teams, which are cohesive units with shared goals, use team effectiveness surveys and feedback from team leaders to pinpoint areas where the team as a whole can improve, such as collaboration or conflict resolution.

2   **Define Objectives:** Clearly define the objectives for each session based on the needs assessment. Objectives should be specific, measurable,

achievable, relevant and time-bound (SMART). This clarity helps in designing exercises that are focused and effective.

3   **Select Appropriate Techniques:** Depending on the objectives, select techniques that best suit the goals. For instance, if the goal is to improve non-verbal communication, design exercises that focus on interpreting the horse's body language.

4   **Incorporate Feedback Mechanisms:** Design the sessions to include immediate feedback for participants. This can be through direct observation of interactions with the horses or through discussions and reflections facilitated by the coach after the exercise.

5   **Iterate Based on Feedback:** Use feedback from participants to refine and adjust exercises. LCH is dynamic, and what works well for one group or individual might not work for another. Be open to making changes based on what is most effective during the sessions.

Safety and Ethical Considerations

When designing new activities in equine-assisted learning, maintaining the safety and welfare of both the participants and the horses is paramount. Here are key considerations to keep in mind:

1   **Participant Safety:** Ensure all participants are briefed on safety protocols around horses. This includes how to approach, touch and lead a horse safely. Provide all necessary safety gear such as helmets and appropriate footwear.

2   **Horse Welfare:** Choose horses that are well-suited to LCH work. They should be calm, well-trained and experienced in working with people. Regular health checks and adequate rest periods between sessions are essential to maintain their well-being.

3   **Ethical Practices:** All LCH activities should adhere to ethical standards that protect the dignity and safety of both humans and animals. Activities should not put horses or participants in situations that could cause distress or danger.

4   **Environment:** Conduct sessions in a controlled environment that is safe for both horses and participants. The area should be free from potential hazards, and there should be adequate space for the activities planned.

5   **Professional Guidance:** Always involve professionals who are trained in both LCH and leadership coaching. This ensures that the sessions are not only safe but also effective in meeting their intended goals.

Design Principles

•   **Objective Alignment:** Ensure each exercise aligns with clear leadership development objectives.

- **Participant Readiness:** Assess the readiness and experience level of participants with horses.
- **Progressive Complexity:** Start with simple exercises and gradually increase complexity as comfort with the horses grows.

Case Studies

- Examples of successful custom sessions designed for different leadership challenges.
- Feedback and outcomes from these sessions to help guide new designs.

Ethical and Safety Guidelines

- Ensuring the well-being of both horses and participants in every session.
- Keeping activities ethical, respectful and focused on positive outcomes for all involved.

Conclusion

- Encouraging ongoing innovation and adaptation in the use of equine-assisted learning for leadership development.

Additional Resources

- Nature Motivation's blog: www.nature-motivation.com/blog.

Appendix II: Leadership Coaching with Horses: Session Planning Worksheet

Section	Details
Coach's Name:	[Coach's Name]
Date:	[Date]
Client's Name:	[Client's Name]
Session Number:	[Session Number]
Location:	[Location]
Session Duration:	[Session Duration]
Session Focus:	State the main objective of the session: What does the client/group or team aim to achieve?
Client Background:	Briefly describe the client's leadership role, challenges and goals.
Coaching Models & Approaches:	Specify which coaching models and approaches will be integrated into this session (e.g., GROW model, NLP, Biofeedback, Psychometric Profiling, Horse-Assisted Coaching).
Session Components:	1 Initial Psychometric Profiling: Utilize results to gain insights into the client's personality traits and behaviors. Discuss how this information will shape the coaching program, including horse interactions.
	2 Biofeedback Integration (Setting Baselines): Employ biofeedback technology to establish physiological baselines during various emotional and cognitive states. Incorporate biofeedback to monitor the client's physiological responses during activities; specify tools used (e.g., heart rate variability).
	3 Goal Setting (GROW Model): G: Goal for this session, R: Reality/context, O: Options/strategies, W: Will/commitment.
	4 NLP Techniques: Use specific NLP techniques (e.g., anchoring, reframing) to address challenges.
	5 Horse Interaction: Outline activities/exercises with the horse(s), including selection, safety precautions and intended outcomes.
	6 Real-Time Feedback: Continue providing physiological data during horse interactions.
	7 Reflective Dialogue: Engage in conversation to explore insights gained during the session.
	8 Feedback and Feedforward: Provide feedback on observed behaviors and discuss improvement strategies.
	9 Data Integration: Analyze both psychometric results and biofeedback data to tailor coaching approaches.
	10 Goal Refinement: Refine leadership goals or action plans based on session insights.
	11 Visualization and Integration: Utilize visualization techniques to help the client integrate their learnings into daily practice.

Section	Details
Key Takeaways:	Summarize main insights, actions or commitments made during the session.
Development Plans / Action Steps:	Assign specific tasks or actions for the client to work on between sessions, aligned with their development goals.
Progress Monitoring:	Continuously monitor physiological responses via biofeedback technology, tracking progress in real-time. Revisit psychometric assessments periodically to measure changes in personality traits and behaviors.
Follow-Up:	Schedule the next coaching session and outline its potential focus based on the progress made during this session.
Coaching Notes:	Record observations, client responses and key discussion points during the session for future reference.

References

American Psychological Association. (2003). Personality changes for the better with age. *Monitor on Psychology*, 34(7), 14. www.apa.org/monitor/julaug03/personality.

Anthony, D. W. (2007). *The horse, the wheel, and language: How Bronze-Age riders from the Eurasian steppes shaped the modern world*. Princeton University Press.

Bachi, K. (2013). Equine-facilitated psychotherapy: The gap in the knowledge and future directions for research. In *Animals and Human Society* (pp. 235–248). Routledge.

Bachi, K. (2013). Equine-facilitated psychotherapy: The gap between practice and knowledge. *Society & Animals*, 20(4), 364–380.

Bachi, K. (2016). *Horse sense for leaders: Building trust-based relationships*. Triarchy Press.

Bachi, K., Terkel, J., & Teichman, M. (2012). Equine reactions to a human grooming approach. *Journal of Veterinary Behavior*, 7(4), 237–243.

Bennett, D. (1998). *Conquerors: The roots of new world horsemanship*. Amigo Publications.

Borghans, L., Duckworth, A. L., Heckman, J. J., & ter Weel, B. (2008). The economics and psychology of personality traits. *The Journal of Human Resources*, 43 (4), 972–1059. www.jstor.org/stable/40057376.

Borsboom, D., & Molenaar, D. (2015). Psychometrics. In J. D. Wright (Ed.), *International encyclopedia of the social & behavioral sciences* (2nd ed.) (pp. 418–422). Elsevier.

Clayton, H. M., & Singleton, W. H. (2002). Ethogram of behaviours observed in horses during trailer loading. *Equine Veterinary Journal*, 34(S34), 140–143.

De Benedittis, A., Marazziti, D., Mandarelli, G., & Lac, V. (2021). Exploring the effects of equine-assisted psychotherapy: A systematic review. *Animals*, 11(2), 487.

Del Giudice, M. J., Yanovsky, B. I., & Finn, S. E. (2014). Personality assessment and feedback practices among executive coaches: In search of a paradigm. *Consulting Psychology Journal: Practice and Research*, 66(3), 155–172. doi:10.1037/cpb0000007.

EAGALA. (2012). *Fundamentals of EAGALA model practice untraining manual* (7th ed.). Equine Assisted Growth and Learning Association.

Gehrke, E. K., Baldwin, A., & Schiltz, P. (2011). Heart rate variability in horses engaged in equine-assisted activities. *Journal of Equine Veterinary Science*, 31(2), 78–84.

Green, E., & Green, A. (1989). *Beyond biofeedback*. Knoll Publishing Company.

Hassett, A. L., Radvanski, D. C., Vaschillo, E. G., Vaschillo, B., Sigal, L. H., Karavidas, M. K., ... & Lehrer, P. M. (2007). A pilot study of the efficacy of heart rate variability (HRV) biofeedback in patients with fibromyalgia. *Applied Psychophysiology and Biofeedback*, 32(1), 1.

Hausberger, M., Roche, H., Henry, S., & Visser, E. K. (2008). A review of the human–horse relationship. *Applied Animal Behaviour Science*, 109(1), 1–24.

Hemmann, K., & Bockisch, F. J. (2015). The skin's role in horse–human tactile communication. *Applied Animal Behaviour Science*, 162, 69–76.

Holt-Lunstad, J., Birmingham, W. A., & Light, K. C. (2008). Influence of a "warm touch" support enhancement intervention among married couples on ambulatory blood pressure, oxytocin, alpha amylase, and cortisol. *Psychosomatic Medicine*, 70 (9), 976–985.

Kim, H.-G., Cheon, E.-J., Bai, D.-S., Lee, Y. H., & Koo, B.-H. (2018). Stress and heart rate variability: A meta-analysis and review of the literature. *Psychiatric Investigation*, 15(3), 235–245.

Ihsan, Z., & Furnham, A. (2018). The new technologies in personality assessment: A review. *Consulting Psychology Journal: Practice and Research*, 70(2). doi:10.1037/cpb0000106.

Jacobson, E. (1929). *Progressive relaxation*. University of Chicago Press.

Jones, J. L. (2008). *Horse brain, human brain: The neuroscience of horsemanship*. Trafalgar Square Books.

Kahneman, D. (2011). *Thinking, fast and slow*. Farrar, Straus and Giroux.

Karimi, S., Ahmadi Malek, F., Yaghoubi Farani, A., & Liobikienė, G. (2023). The role of transformational leadership in developing innovative work behaviors: The mediating role of employees' psychological capital. *Sustainability*, 15(2), 1267. doi:10.3390/su15021267.

Kerr, C. E., Sacchet, M. D., Lazar, S. W., Moore, C. I., & Jones, S. R. (2011). Mindfulness starts with the body: Somatosensory attention and top-down modulation of cortical alpha rhythms in mindfulness meditation. *Frontiers in Human Neuroscience*, 5, 1–15.

King, C. E., & Hemsworth, P. H. (2020). Horse–human interactions and the effect on the behaviour and welfare of horses. *Applied Animal Behaviour Science*, 234, 105168.

Kohanov, L. (2003). *The Tao of Equus: A woman's journey of healing and transformation through the way of the horse*. New World Library.

Küssner, M. B. (2017). Eysenck's theory of personality and the role of background music in cognitive task performance: A mini-review of conflicting findings and a new perspective. *Frontiers in Psychology*, 8, 1991. doi:10.3389/fpsyg.2017.01991.

Laborde, S., Mosley, E., & Thayer, J. F. (2017). Heart rate variability and cardiac vagal tone in psychophysiological research: Recommendations for experiment planning, data analysis, and data reporting. *Frontiers in Psychology*, 8, 213.

Laborde, S., Mosley, E., & Thayer, J. F. (2017). Heart rate variability and cardiac vagal tone in psychophysiological research: Recommendations for experiment planning, data analysis, and data reporting. *Frontiers in Psychology*, 8, 213.

Lapsley, D., & Ste, P. C. (2012). *Id, ego, and superego*. University of Notre Dame. doi:10.1016/B978-0-12-375000-6.00199-3.

MacDonald, K. B. (1988). *Social and personality development: An evolutionary synthesis*. SpringerLink. https://link.springer.com/book/10.1007/978-1-4757-0292-7.

McCraty, R., & Zayas, M. A. (2014). Cardiac coherence, self-regulation, autonomic stability, and psychosocial well-being. *Frontiers in Psychology*, 5, 1090.

Mehrabian, A. (2017). *Nonverbal communication*. Routledge.

Nightingale, S. T. (2010). *El Maestro equino: coaching, psicoterapia y aprendizaje asistido con equinos*. El mundo de las terapias.

Ponzo, V., Kubiak, T., & Kossowska, M. (2018). Neuroscience of communication—Part 2: Mimicry and "theory of mind." *Journal of Education, Culture and Society*, 1 (2), 113–124.

Proops, L., & McComb, K. (2013). Attributing attention: The use of human-given cues by domestic horses (*Equus caballus*). *Animal Cognition*, 16(2), 197–205.

Rauen, J. E. (2017). *The effects of equine assisted learning on emotional intelligence competencies and leadership skills*. Eastern Kentucky University Honors Theses Student Scholarship. https://encompass.eku.edu/honors_theses.

Reiner, R. (2008). Integrating a portable biofeedback device into clinical practice for patients with anxiety disorders: Results of a pilot study. *Applied Psychophysiology and Biofeedback*, 33(1), 55–61.

Reisfield, G. M., & Wilson, G. R. (2004). Use of metaphor in the discourse on cancer. *Journal of Clinical Oncology*, 22(19). doi:10.1200/JCO.2004.03.136.

Rizzolatti, G., Fogassi, L., & Gallese, V. (1996). Functional MRI evidence for mirror neuron activity in the human brain. *Journal Neuron*, 13(2), 375–382.

Rizzolatti, G., & Sinigaglia, C. (2010). The functional role of the parieto-frontal mirror circuit: Interpretations and misinterpretations. *Nature Reviews Neuroscience*, 11(4), 264–274.

Rizzolatti, G., & Sinigaglia, C. (2016). The mirror mechanism: A basic principle of brain function. *Nature Reviews Neuroscience*, 17(12), 757–765.

Roberts, M. (1996). *The man who listens to horses*. Random House.

Schwartz, M. S., & F. Andrasik. (2003) *Biofeedback: A practitioner's guide* (3rd ed.). Guilford Press.

Slayton, S. C., Bozentka, A. B., & Petersen, N. S. (2016). Equine-assisted psychotherapy: A descriptive study. *Journal of Creativity in Mental Health*, 11(1), 104–116.

Smith, A. V., Proops, L., Grounds, K., Wathan, J., & McComb, K. (2016). Functionally relevant responses to human facial expressions of emotion in the domestic horse. *Biology Letters*, 12(2). doi:10.1098/rsbl.2015.0907.

Smith, L. B., Cipriani, D., & Shklovskiy, G. M. (2019). Quantifying heart rate variability using smartphone-based photoplethysmography. *Journal of Medical Engineering & Technology*, 43(4), 269–279.

Soto, C. J. (2018). Big Five personality traits. In M. H. Bornstein (Ed.), *The Sage encyclopedia of lifespan human development* (pp. 240–241). Sage Publications.

Stein, R., Swan, A. B., & Eureka College. (2019). Evaluating the validity of Myers-Briggs Type Indicator theory: A teaching tool and window into intuitive psychology. *Social and Personality Psychology Compass*, 13(2), e12434. doi:10.1111/spc3.12434.

Thayer, J. F., & Lane, R. D. (2000). A model of neurovisceral integration in emotion regulation and dysregulation. *Journal of Affective Disorders*, 61(3), 201–216.

Index

For Product Safety Concerns and Information please contact our EU
representative GPSR@taylorandfrancis.com
Taylor & Francis Verlag GmbH, Kaufingerstraße 24, 80331 München, Germany